Family & Parenthood
Policy & Practice

Young single mothers: barriers to independent living

**Suzanne Speak,
Stuart Cameron,
Roberta Woods and
Rose Gilroy**

PUBLISHED BY

**Family
Policy
Studies
Centre**

SUPPORTED BY

JOSEPH
ROWNTREE
FOUNDATION

Published by Family Policy Studies Centre,
231 Baker Street, London NW1 7XE.
Tel: 0171 486 8179

ISBN 0 907051 85 5

July 1995

© FPSC/JRF

SUPPORTED BY

JOSEPH
ROWNTREE
FOUNDATION

Design and print by Intertype

Contents

Acknowledgements

Many people helped in the production of this report. In particular the authors would like to thank the young mothers, who spoke so freely and openly about their lives. Also to be thanked for their assistance and comments are the many support workers who were involved in the study, especially health visitors.

Special thanks go to the Joseph Rowntree Foundation for funding the study, and especially Jackie Wilkins of the Foundation, for her support and encouragement throughout.

Suzanne Speak
July 1995

Introduction

This research project has its origins in Newcastle Gingerbread's need for practical information to develop its services and facilities for young single mothers.

In the early 1990s workers at Gingerbread noticed a change in the characteristics of lone parents visiting the Gingerbread centre in Newcastle and using its services. In earlier days, service users tended to be in their late twenties or older, and 'lone' parents as a result of a relationship breakdown, with very few unmarried and truly single mothers seeking support. However, in more recent years the organisation has noted an increase in the number of single (never-married or cohabiting) mothers seeking advice. Furthermore, the average age of the single mothers tended to be lower than that of other 'lone' mothers.

Whereas older divorced or separated mothers had generally displayed a range of emotional and financial problems relating to the breakdown of their relationships, maintenance or custody battles, the younger single mothers who were beginning to approach the organisation for support were displaying a different range of problems. Most noticeable were problems relating to establishing an independent home on leaving the family home or other accommodation. The problems ranged from difficulty in accessing suitable housing to problems in finding funds for furniture to turn a property into a home. Many young women, having been offered a property by the local authority, were having great difficulty moving in and maintaining their new independence for any length of time.

The Newcastle Gingerbread Trust was eager to develop services and facilities aimed at assisting this subgroup of lone mothers with their transition to independent living. It appeared to workers at the Trust that no group experienced greater difficulty with this transition than those leaving supported accommodation.

There has been an increase in recent years in the development of supported housing schemes and hostels for young unmarried mothers. This development is likely to continue, possibly encouraged by the Government's new thinking on homelessness, suggesting the use of purpose built hostels for young mothers and their babies.[1] However, little is known about the housing circumstances of mothers once they leave such hostels, or indeed their own family homes, and become independent householders in their own right.

The need for this investigation

Despite the Government's undertaking to reduce the number of conceptions to very young teenage single women by the year 2000, there is still likely to be a considerable number of young women raising their children alone. These mothers represent the changing face of lone parents.

No agency, statutory or voluntary, can hope to keep pace with the changing problems and prospects of its clients without detailed knowledge of their lives, needs and aspirations. A detailed study of the living standards of young single mothers is important in order to fully understand in what ways their social and material circumstances fall short of an acceptable norm, how their children's lives are restricted as a result and how they might be best helped to provide an adequate home for their children. Whether society is prepared or able to provide this help may be another matter. Furthermore it is important to understand the sometimes limited quality of life these young mothers and their children are able to achieve at the present time, otherwise we may find ourselves continuing with policies which could in fact lead to even greater poverty and social exclusion.

Set within the context of rising numbers of lone parents and increasing concern over their need for state benefit and local authority housing, this study looks at the difficulties faced by young single mothers as they endeavour to establish a first independent home, without the aid of a partner.

In the 20 year period from 1971, the number of lone parents in Britain rose from 380,000 to 1,040,000, not counting lone fathers or widows.[2] One group, unmarried lone mothers, has increased at a faster rate than any other, from

90,000, 15.8 percent of the total in 1971, to 390,000, 33 per cent of the total in 1991.[3] Within this fastest growing subgroup of lone mothers, particular attention has focused on teenage single mothers. Whilst births outside marriage to teenage women have fallen as a percentage of all births outside marriage, from 34 per cent in 1979 to 22 per cent in 1990,[4] what has increased is the likelihood of such births resulting in single lone motherhood, rather than a shot-gun wedding or cohabitation.[5] This change has resulted in a growing number of teenage women needing to establish themselves as independent house-holders in order to provide a home for their children.

A number of changes to social security and housing policy have taken place which have made this process more difficult in recent years, and proposed further changes may compound these difficulties.

The Social Security Act 1988 brought about one of the major changes affecting teenage single mothers: the raising of the threshold for income support from 16 to 18 years of age, unless a young woman has a child. This coincided with the introduction of the Youth Training Programme, and together these changes put some very young single pregnant women in a difficult position. They are unable to make a claim for income support, as they do not have a child, yet may have extreme difficulty in finding suitable YTS placements given their condition. Even once income support can be claimed, it is paid at a lower rate to those under 18 years of age.

The 1988 Act also saw the abolition of the single payment which had been used to help a young person acquire the basics to set up home. This was replaced by the social fund for those in receipt of income support. However, no claim can be made from the social fund until the claimant has been on income support for 26 weeks, further adding to the difficulties.

The early nineties saw the introduction of the Child Support Agency, with its power to levy financial penalties on lone mother benefit claimants who withhold information about the fathers of their children.

As will be shown, teenage single women are heavily reliant on local authority housing. This housing is becoming less available as new construction has virtually ended and many suitable properties are lost through 'Right to Buy'. It may become even less available for young single mothers if proposals to increase the use of mother and baby hostels are fully developed into policy.[6]

Many of the housing and social security policies affecting lone parents today have their roots in the past. From the Poor Law Commissioners of the nineteenth century to the Finer Committee on One Parent Families in 1974, policy-makers have had difficulty providing for this 'special group', as the Finer report referred to lone parents. Those benefits which are available to support lone parents today do not differentiate between the many subgroups of lone parents and their differing needs, except in their different treatment of widows.[7]

Whilst it may be argued that many of the problems faced by lone parents are those faced by anyone living on a low income, this report will show that within Finer's 'special group' there is an 'even more special group', who have greater difficulty in establishing and maintaining independent living. The difficulties young mothers have in providing a secure and suitable home for their children need to be identified if social policy is to address them.

Objectives

The aims of the research were to investigate the barriers to independent living, as experienced by a young, single, never-married mother, setting up her first independent home, without the financial or practical assistance of a partner.

Given the recent controversy over teenage single parenthood the target group for the study was women between the ages of 16 and 24 years, who had never been married, were not cohabiting, and who had given birth to their first child before the age of 20. The women were either living independently or trying to set up an independent home.

Housing is only one piece in the jigsaw of independence. Having acquired a house or flat, a mother needs finance, furniture and support in order to turn it into an independent home. Given that many of the mothers are reliant on social housing *and* social support, the aims of the research were to identify how well the current housing markets – local authority, housing associations, or private – together with the current benefit structure, enable a young single mother to establish a secure and safe home in which to raise her child.

With continued cuts in social spending and an increasing work-load on social services, it was hoped to examine the role of the voluntary sector in providing support in the form of self-help groups, advice agencies and community groups.

The aims, then, could be seen as seeking answers to the following main questions:

- How easy or difficult is it for a young single mother to find suitable housing?

- What is the cost in real terms of furnishing and equipping a home, and how is this achieved?

- How well do the existing benefits structure, housing and support systems in the region assist a young mother in maintaining a stable home environment in future years?

The area

Newcastle upon Tyne

The research centred on the city of Newcastle upon Tyne, where there were 6,593 lone parent households in 1991, an increase of 3,991 in the 10 years from 1981.[8] No statistics are available for the numbers of single, never-married mothers within this total.

There are a number of large peripheral estates around the city, displaying the problems of urban deprivation, such as high crime rates, vandalism, poor-quality difficult-to-let housing and high unemployment.

The voluntary and community sector is active across the city, and much community development work has taken place. This has been restricted in recent years by the cutting of social services grant aid to such organisations by £300,000 over the five-year period to April 1994. The Government did accept the 1991 bid for City Challenge money for the regeneration of the west-end of the city; however, the 1992 east-end bid was not successful.

As with other larger cities, some neighbourhoods in Newcastle have an excess of housing. Those willing to accept property in these areas experience little delay.

To a certain extent, this may challenge the idea of young single women getting pregnant deliberately in order to jump the housing queue, since, for those who are less choosy about their property or its location, there is no queue to jump.

The situation for young mothers in Newcastle is likely to be similar to that of mothers in any large city. However, more rural areas might well display interesting contrasts. For this reason it was decided to include a smaller scale study of two areas in the rural hinterland of Newcastle: Castle Morpeth and Blyth Valley (see Figure 1).

Figure 1 Newcastle and its hinterland

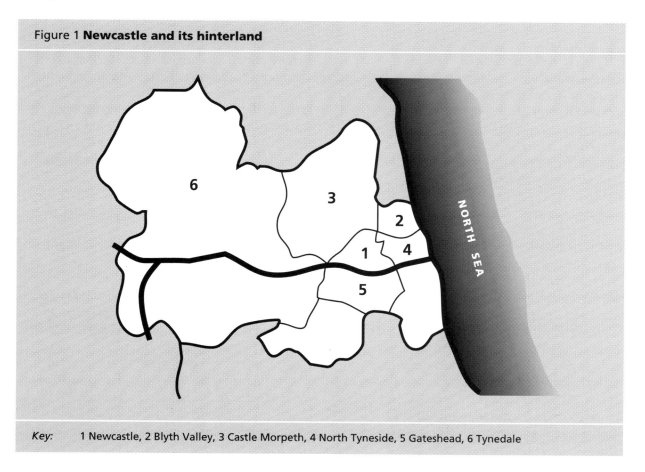

Key: 1 Newcastle, 2 Blyth Valley, 3 Castle Morpeth, 4 North Tyneside, 5 Gateshead, 6 Tynedale

Castle Morpeth

Castle Morpeth is a rural ex-mining area. The area had a total of 5,884 households with dependent children in 1991,494 of which were lone parent households, more than double the 1981 figure of 209.[9] Of the 494, 239 lived in local authority accommodation, 41 lived in private rented accommodation and only seven in housing association property.

The area has a total of 3,469 local authority properties, having lost 1,306 since 'Right to Buy' legislation came into force. There has been no 'general needs' council property built since 1981. The majority of local authority housing is concentrated in the larger urban areas of Morpeth and Ponteland, and is generally in a good condition, with much smaller clusters of council property in smaller more outlying towns. There is limited private rented accommodation, including privately let ex-miners houses and farm cottages both in Morpeth and Ponteland and in some of the more rural villages.

Facilities and services are heavily concentrated in the main towns, and there is very limited voluntary sector or community development activity, other than on the main local authority estates. Public transport services are generally good in Morpeth and Ponteland but very poor to the rural outposts.

Blyth Valley

Blyth Valley is less rural than Castle Morpeth and, having been predominantly a mining area, is now suffering heavily, in terms of rising unemployment, from the decline in the mining industry in recent years. The area is considerably smaller than Castle Morpeth, yet has almost twice the number of households with dependent children (10,641) and three times the number of lone parent households, with 1,519 in total in 1991, having increased from 557 at the 1981 census.[10]

The local authority has lost 2,895 properties since 'Right to Buy', and its remaining housing stock of 8,506 units is heavily concentrated in the two main towns of Cramlington and Blyth. Within Blyth local authority housing is located predominantly on one estate, Cowpen, which holds approximately 1,500 of the town's 2,000 local authority properties. There are clusters of local authority properties in the smaller areas of Seaton Sluice and Seaton Delaval. Property is in a generally good condition across the area. Two main housing associations, North British and Home Housing Association Ltd (formerly North

Housing Association), operate, mainly in Blyth and Cramlington, and 167 lone parent families live in housing association property in the Blyth Valley area.[11]

Methodology

Recruiting the sample

The main sample for individual interview consisted of 40 mothers who fitted the criteria (as defined on p. 6) exactly, 20 from Newcastle and 10 each from Castle Morpeth and Blyth Valley. Apart from the fact that finding many more mothers who fitted the criteria would have been difficult, it was felt that, given the in-depth nature of the inteviews to be carried out, this was a suitable number.

To get as diverse a sample of mothers as possible, it was decided to recruit the mothers through health visitors in each area wherever possible. Virtually all mothers and expectant mothers have regular contact with a health visitor, initially for ante-natal classes during pregnancy and then for support after the birth. This contact lasts throughout the child's first months, with regular baby weighing sessions, infant health checks and vaccinations. Health visitors are the key players in the support of all new mothers using the national health service.

A shorter route to accessing a sample of young single mothers might have been to visit community centres and support groups; however, this might have resulted in only accessing those mothers motivated enough to visit such organisations. It might have limited the sample further to only those areas of the city where such initiatives have been established. Health visitors, on the other hand, hold clinics in all areas of the city, allowing, in theory, access to mothers in both working-class and middle-class districts.

However, the very low number of births to single teenage women in Castle Morpeth – only 22 registered in 1992 – made it difficult to contact women in this area who fitted the criteria. For this reason, few of the Castle Morpeth mothers were contacted via health visitors, and other methods had to be used, including local press articles.

Attempts to achieve a balanced sample of mothers from all socio–economic backgrounds (to ascertain whether the problems experienced by young single mothers were class-related) proved difficult. Despite their willingness to assist, the health visitors from the more middle-class districts did not come forward with names of young single mothers, whereas those from the inner city estates had many names to offer. Local GPs were approached to see if mothers in the less-disadvantaged areas were some how by-passing health visitors and using only their own family doctor, and whether the number of conceptions to teenage girls in their area might be increasing.

Doctors in the less-disadvantaged areas were not aware of a great number of conceptions, whereas in the inner city areas doctors identified it as a specific and growing problem. In reality, it appears that the mothers did tend to come from the less-well-off, traditionally working-class areas of the city. This may not reflect the national picture of births to single teenage girls. This wider picture is difficult to establish as data relating to live births or terminations to single teenage women does not take into account socio–economic background.

Not all the mothers in the sample were living in their own homes at the time of the interview, although the majority – 31 out of 40 – were. Of the others, five were living with their families, two were living in supported accommodation and one was living with friends. Only one mother was living in a homeless persons unit, awaiting a property. At the time of the study, no mothers could be found living in temporary bed and breakfast accommodation in the study areas. This was both promising and surprising, given that in England in 1990 over 10,000 households, mainly headed by lone mothers, were living in such situations.[12] It is also notable that in North Tyneside, an adjacent local authority, there were 190 lone parents, including young single mothers, in bed and breakfast accommodation between March 1993 and February 1994. Here mothers endured an average wait of four months in temporary accommodation.

The methods

Interviews with mothers

In all, 40 individual, semi-structured interviews were conducted by the authors with women who strictly fitted the criteria. The interviews were in two parts. The first part centred on a questionnaire and lasted approximately one hour. On completion of the questionnaire, there followed a period of open discussion, which sometimes included other women, friends, sisters or support workers. Interviews took place in clinics, in community centres and in the mothers' own homes. Although the mothers who were interviewed displayed great willingness to talk

openly about all aspects of their lives, the actual success rate for contacting the mothers referred by health visitors was poor. Less than one in five referrals got to the interview stage. Even when an interview had been agreed to, and a date set by the mother, the interviewer often found no one at home when she called.

In addition to the individual interviews, there were 15 guided group discussions with lone mothers, including divorced, separated and single women who were all raising their children alone and already met at centres such as Gingerbread and the National Children's Home Day Centre in Newcastle. Both the group discussions and the interviews concentrated on the efforts of the young single mothers to find, set up and maintain an independent home, and the differences between their situation and that of other lone mothers. Why they were on their own rather than cohabiting or married, and how they came to be single mothers in the first place, was not relevant to this research.

Quotations used in this report are all taken from either the individual interviews or the group discussions conducted, as described above, as part of this study. Data collected for the project are referenced as The Newcastle Study, 1994.

Notes to introduction

1 Department of the Environment (1994). *Access to Local Authority and Housing Association Tenancies, Consultation Paper.* HMSO (London)

2 OPCS Statistics also 1981, 1991 Census data - Office of Population Census and Statistics. HMSO (London)

3 *Ibid*

4 Office of Population Censuses and Surveys (1991). *Population Trends No. 65.* HMSO (London)

5 Burghes, L. and Brown, M. (1995, forthcoming). *Single Mothers: problems, prospects and policies.* Family Policy Study Centre (London)

6 Department of the Environment. (1994). (note 1)

7 See for example Brown, J.C. (1982). *In Search of a Policy* National Council of One Parent Families (London)

8 National Census data, 1981 and 1991, OPCS (London)

9 *Ibid*

10 *Ibid*

11 *Ibid*

12 Department of the Environment (1991). *Homeless Statistics.* HMSO (London); see also Greve, J. (1991). *Homeless in Britain.* Joseph Rowntree Foundation (York)

Part I
The barriers to establishing independent living

A two-part game of snakes and ladders

What was initially a study of the problems faced by young single mothers when they first tried to establish an independent home, developed into a wider investigation into the continued difficulties in maintaining that independence. Discussions with mothers revealed the often turbulent nature of their lives during the first few years of independence. Central to the study was the need to identify to what extent the first home, and difficulties in establishing what the mothers perceived to be a comfortable and pleasant standard of living, were responsible for any later instability. How did a young mother's satisfaction with her first home, the cost and standard of furnishings, her income, and the support she received relate to her future 'career' and satisfaction as an independent householder?

In this report we therefore discuss the barriers to independence in two sections: Part I looks at the problems in establishing an independent household, while Part II discusses the difficulties in maintaining an independent living of the desired standard. Chapter 1 concerns the decision to establish an independent home, Chapter 2 is on the acquisition of a property, Chapter 3 looks at furnishing a first home, Chapter 4 looks at the financial aspects, Chpater 5 considers the available support and Chapter 6 offers some concluding remarks on Part I.

Background information

The role of age

In an examination of the situation of women between the ages of 16 and 24, it might be expected that age would play a major role in their stability. It appears, however, from the evidence both of the mothers themselves, and those professionals working to support them, that age is by no means the most important factor. Research suggests that maturity is not directly linked to age. Some very young mothers, who gave birth before the age of 16, were found to have few housing problems and to be coping well once they had made the transition to independence some months or years later; whilst other mothers, who did not give birth until 18 or 19, were not necessarily either better prepared or less likely to encounter fewer problems.

It may be that the increased support given to the very young mothers was instrumental in preparing them for independence, especially those who continued with their education at the Ashlyns Centre for Schoolgirl Mothers, Newcastle. It is likely also that the tendency of the very young to remain within the family home for some time after the birth plays a part. Except for the two major factors of income and access to housing, the difficulties a mother faces when first trying to acquire and set up a home are the same regardless of age. Once the transition has been made, and independent tenancy achieved, income remains the only age-related barrier to maintaining it, and this too should disappear after the age of 18, when income support is paid at the upper rate.

The role of route to independence

For any young person, the route to housing independence can be thought of as a line from family home to first independent tenancy. In the case of young single mothers, this line is crossed by two significant events, pregnancy and birth. It would appear that the housing and support situations surrounding these two events have great bearing on the ability of a mother to establish and maintain her first independent home.

Despite their very diverse family backgrounds and upbringings, the mothers in the study had all travelled, or were travelling, one of four basic routes to their first homes. Some had left home prior to pregnancy, and were living alone or with friends or boyfriends, some left home due to pregnancy, some remained within the family until the birth, and some remained there for some time after the birth.

With some exceptions, those who remained in the family home throughout their pregnancy and for some time after the birth were better prepared once they made the transition than were those who had left prior to pregnancy or because of it.

The lack of affordable accommodation for young single people means that many young women who leave home during their teen years find themselves moving from one temporary home to another, perhaps staying with friends, boyfriends or other family members. One young woman had lived at 12 different addresses between leaving home at 16, and her first pregnancy at the age of 18, at which time she moved into a supported mother and baby hostel. Others who became pregnant during this transient period had lived under similar situations. Some were fortunate to be welcomed back into the family home, their new-found status even helping to repair the rift in family relations. Others felt it was the straw that broke the camel's back. When it became impossible for them to remain with friends, they moved to supported mother and baby accommodation.

The women who were the least well equipped to live alone, despite considerable help in setting up their first home, were the six mothers who had spent time in supported mother and baby hostels. This finding is consistent with a study by The Trust for the Study of Adolescence, which highlights the difficulty such young women face on leaving supported accommodation.[1]

"I wanted to [leave the hostel], couldn't wait me. But then when you're on your own it's different. No one to talk to all the day, no money and that. At least here [mother and baby hostel] there's other Mams and you can put the bairn down and know some one else will watch on like for a few minutes. Yeh ... it's hard if you don't have no one. That's why I'm back here all the time, can't bloody get rid of me now!"

It should be noted that, in many cases, this difficulty probably reflects the sometimes extreme, long-term problems of many of the young women in hostels, especially the total loss of family support, rather than any failure on the part of the hostel workers. This problem has been recognised by Castle Morpeth Social Services, now trying to develop more appropriate, inter-agency support services for young people leaving care, of whom a number are young mothers or pregnant young women.

Barriers to acquiring a first independent home

Housing

Despite the widespread popular belief that teenage girls get pregnant deliberately in order to jump the housing queue, the Department of the Environment's own figures for 1991 show just 0.3 per cent (13,000) of heads of council homes to be women under 20.[2]

Addressing homelessness, or the threat of homelessness, as a route to permanent council housing, the DOE has referred to 'the abuse to which the present arrangements are subject'.[3] A survey of local authorities by the Chartered Institute of Housing showed that, across the 30 authorities which responded, between two and 14 per cent of those presenting themselves as homeless were teenage mothers.[4] The survey showed no evidence of lone parents being treated more favourably than two parent households. In general, lone mothers in local authority accommodation tended to be older women who had separated from their partners.

If local authority property is no more readily available to young single mothers, under normal circumstances, than to other families, what then are their options when it comes to acquiring a first home and how long can they expect to wait?

Among lone parents in Newcastle 17.5 per cent either own or are buying their homes, but the proportion of these who fit the criteria for this study is likely to be very low, with only 6 per cent of single, never-married mothers, *nationally*, being owner-occupiers. Only one of the mothers in this study owned her own home. Discounting home ownership, there are three main avenues open to a young single mother once she decides to set out on the path to independent householder status. These are:

(i)   Local authority housing;

(ii) Housing association property;

(iii) Private rented property.

Which avenue offers the greatest chance of success depends on several factors, including a lone mother's age, the level of housing association activity in the area, and the extent of private sector property. These three will be looked at separately in the following sections.

Local authority

Nationally lone parents are more likely than married or cohabiting couples to live in local authority accommodation. This likelihood increases for single, never-married mothers, with 80 per cent living in local authority property against just under 60 per cent of divorced or separated mothers.[5] In Newcastle 4,415 lone parent householders, just under 67 per cent, are local authority tenants.[6] However, it is not possible to identify what proportion of these are young single mothers and what proportion are separated or divorced parents. It is possible to say, however, that, for the vast majority of young mothers in this study, the local authority is seen as the major provider of secure housing. Of the 31 mothers in the study trying to rent accommodation independently, 30 had applied to the local authority, only 14 had tried a housing association and six had approached private landlords. Three had also tried other means of renting accommodation, such as friends or family. In the end, 25 of the 31 took up council tenancies for their first independent home.

Two routes to local authority housing

Like some other large cities, Newcastle has an excess of social housing, a percentage of which is difficult to let, as there has been a continuing decline in the state of Newcastle's housing stock over many years. This decline is reflected in the city's Housing Investment Program bids, with current estimates for 1994 being upwards of 4,000 difficult-to-let-and-manage properties in the city.

Because of the number of vacant properties available, although many families spend several months or years on the housing department waiting list for property in a more desirable area, the less choosy or those with urgent housing need are often offered a tenancy with little delay and without recourse to temporary accommodation, such as bed and breakfast or homeless units. This surplus of housing, together with changes in allocations and rehousing policy, has resulted in the cutting of the city's temporary accommodation bill from more than £300,000 in 1990/91 to approximately £10,000 in 1993/4.

The waiting list route

How long a mother waited before being offered a tenancy depended not only on age and circumstances but also on the allocations policy of the area she was living in. There were noticeable differences between the city of Newcastle and the surrounding areas of Castle Morpeth and Blyth Valley. The three authorities all operate very similar waiting lists and point systems: points are awarded for where facilities are shared or lacking and for spatial requirements.

All three authorities will accept applications from people between 16 and 18 years of age, but will normally only offer a licence, rather than a tenancy, to someone under 18 years, and only then in exceptional circumstances. It is in their interpretation of, and response to, 'exceptional circumstances' that they differ. Where there is no immediate, urgent housing need, a mother will have to wait her turn on the list. The length of wait depends very much on the desirability of the area she requests and the points she might be awarded for overcrowding in the family home. In Newcastle, a mother with few overcrowding points, wanting a more desirable area, can expect to wait several years. In less desirable areas, she may wait a few months or less. Of the eight Newcastle mothers living in council property who had not been classed as homeless, three waited over two years, four waited between six months and one year and another waited 18 months. Two women, having been told they could expect to wait at least two years, gave up and found private rented accommodation.

The picture of lengthy waits repeats itself in Blyth Valley and Castle Morpeth, where in some of the more desirable areas up to 90 per cent of local authority property has been lost through 'Right to Buy', thus lengthening the wait for a property in these areas and concentrating those with urgent need in less desirable neighbourhoods.

The homeless route

Homelessness as a route to a local authority tenancy was the cause of much controversy during the early 1990s. However, homelessness is not necessarily rooflessness. Although nine of the 31 independent mothers had been classed as homeless prior to being given a tenancy, only two had been in temporary accommodation. The remaining seven were living in unsuitable conditions within the family home, and were threatened with imminent homelessness.

It is possible that a number of young mothers, faced with many months or years on the housing waiting list, do collude with their parents to speed up the process by suggesting they might be made homeless unless a property is found quickly. However, only one of the sample mothers admitted to this, and she had been waiting for 15 months by that time.

"They [the housing department] weren't doing owt. I'd been waiting for months, over a year and there wasn't room like, not really 'cause me and Jenny [sister] shared, so then there was three of us with the baby. In the end my Mam said they'd have to give me a place, 'cause it were getting her down as well, and my Dad. So she wrote and told them that I couldn't stay no longer, that she'd turn me out. I don't think she would have like, not really."

Newcastle, because of its excess of social housing, is in a position to respond quickly to the urgent housing needs of some young mothers who find themselves homeless, or threatened with homelessness, without the need to resort to temporary accommodation. Whether this quick response is necessarily beneficial in the long term is questionable, and will be looked into at a later stage.

Does this speedy provision of housing for homeless mothers in Newcastle incite them to engineer their homeless status in order to 'jump the housing queue', as some suspect? John Greve, in *Homeless in Britain,* points out that, while lone parents are over represented in the figures of those accepted as homeless by local authorities, by far the majority have experienced the breakdown of a marriage or other partnership. Only a very small percentage are teenage girls. Further doubt is cast on this suspicion of engineered homelessness, if we look at the circumstances of the seven women from the Newcastle sample who were classed as homeless when they took up their first tenancies. Five of the seven had applied for council housing under the normal waiting list points system. Four of these were living in temporary but satisfactory accommodation, two with friends and two in supported hostels, under the watchful eye of social services. The fifth was living with her mother and believed she could stay there as long as necessary.

The two women living in hostel accommodation had applied for a council property well in advance of their proposed leaving date, one prior to pregnancy. When the time came for them to leave the hostel they were offered housing immediately, under the homeless legislation. By this time they had each been on the waiting list for over six months.

The two living with friends had applied to be housed under the points system when they moved into their friend's homes, at some point during their pregnancies. Their housing urgency arose when they could no longer remain with friends after the birth of their babies, some three to six months later:

"Well it didn't work out how we'd hoped. We're still friends but living together, it were difficult. There wasn't room, we were on top of each other all the time, getting on each other's nerves. There was me and her [daughter] and Emma and her two, it were just too much. I didn't think it would take so long. I don't think Emma would have said to come and stay if she'd known it were going to take so long. So I had to leave, it were best really."

The fifth woman had lived with her mother throughout her pregnancy and expected to remain there as long as she wanted. She applied to be housed when the baby was born. As is common, the arrival of the baby caused more stress than anticipated and her mother told her to leave sooner than intended. Threatened with homelessness she was housed three months later, nine months after she first applied.

But for unforeseen events, these women would all have happily waited their turn on the housing department list and fully intended to do so when they first applied.

Two of the original seven 'homeless' mothers in Newcastle had not applied for council property. They were both living with their families and believed they could continue to do so. Their homeless status arose due to abuse in the family home. Their applications for housing were supported by local social services.

Nothing from the study gave any evidence to suggest that any of the women had become pregnant deliberately in order to jump a housing queue. None had intended to become independent of their families at that point in their lives. Pregnancy had not been used as a means to independence; rather, it had thrust independence upon them.

The use of temporary accommodation

The situation for young mothers classed as homeless in the more rural area of Blyth Valley is quite different. The lack of council property and the much lower turnover in tenancies means that there is a far greater chance of a young mother being placed in temporary accommodation prior to being offered a permanent property. In Blyth, a mother can expect to wait on average 4–6 weeks in the homeless families unit before being offered permanent housing.

There was no evidence that this difficulty in acquiring council housing in the surrounding areas tempted young mothers to migrate to the city. Indeed, the mothers from the more rural areas tended to want to move even shorter distances from their families than did the city mothers. Furthermore, it is common for mothers waiting in temporary accommodation to give up and return to their family home or a friend's home. It would seem that the isolation and removal of support networks, together with poor and expensive public transport, causes too great a strain. There is a feeling amongst some health and social workers that temporary accommodation, in some areas, is used in this way as a deterrent.

Mothers who do wait their time in temporary accommodation are eventually made one offer of a property, which they are obliged to accept, unless they have reasonable grounds for refusing. This one-offer rule applies to those housed via the homeless route in all three areas, whether in temporary accommodation or not. A young mother can refuse a property but, unless she can prove it to be unsuitable, she will not be offered another and will be placed at the bottom of the waiting list. Unfortunately, few young mothers under pressure to leave their existing homes, and in some cases living under very difficult conditions, have enough self-confidence to challenge the housing department on the suitability of a property. They might be more inclined to do so if the temporary accommodation available in some areas was of a better standard. This difficulty in refusing a property, and the stigma attached to most temporary accommodation, has the effect of pushing young single mothers into accepting property in less desirable areas, which they are not happy with, and which in many cases is clearly unsatisfactory.

Some young women do refuse a property because they perceive it to be unsuitable, others simply because it is not what they want or it is in an area they do not wish to live in. In such cases, the mother might be offered a few weeks temporary accommodation to allow her to find alternative housing, perhaps in the private sector. More often she will return to her family home. Several cases of this nature were reported in the more rural areas but none in Newcastle.

In reality, a mother and child should never be literally roofless, as, under the terms of the Children Act 1989, social services have a duty to secure accommodation for any child in need.[7] The three years following the Act saw a difficult period, when, in some areas, homeless mothers with young children were passed backwards and forwards between social services and housing departments, each claiming the mother and children to be the other's responsibility. The duty was reaffirmed as lying with social services in mid 1994.

The most noticeable difference between the city of Newcastle and the contrasting areas of Blyth Valley and Castle Morpeth was in the use of different types of temporary accommodation. In Newcastle, the only mothers in any form of temporary accommodation were those in charitably run mother and baby hostels, such as the Girls Friendly Society hostel or Catholic Care. They were there for a combination of reasons, mainly relating to family breakdown, not merely their own homelessness. In the other two areas, mothers frequently spent time in general homeless families accommodation, rather than in hostels. Whilst a stay in mother and baby accommodation brings with it the advantage of support from experienced workers and peers, homeless families accommodation provides little more than a safe roof.

There may, however, be benefits, for both the housing department and the mothers, from the use of homeless accommodation. First it may be that the use of temporary accommodation in these areas acts as a deterrent to young women applying as homeless, thus ensuring that they remain on the waiting list, unless the situation at home is completely intolerable. The advantages of this for the local authority are clear. However, given the difficulties young mothers face with the one-offer rule when housed as homeless, and the benefits to be gained from remaining for a longer period in the family home, mothers too might benefit from this deterrent. There are obvious exceptions to this, and the extremely difficult, if not dangerous situations, some young mothers are forced to endure in the family home must not be overlooked.

Second, for those who are not deterred, placing a young woman and her child in temporary accommodation brings her to the notice of other agencies and workers. This in itself may make her slightly less vulnerable to being placed in an unsuitable situation, and allows for some intervention and control over her situation by support workers.

Satisfaction with the first home

Regardless of whether a tenancy has been achieved from the waiting list or the homeless route, many mothers are disappointed with the condition of their first home. Although few of the study mothers reported that major repairs were required, the majority said it took considerable time and effort to clean, prepare and possibly decorate their new home to a standard suitable for a young child before they could move in.

For some mothers, living at home with their parents, this delay in moving in caused no problem. It provided them with time to collect furnishings and to decorate, even have carpets fitted. In some cases, the whole family rallied round to help:

"... not till I get me place more how I want it. You should have seen the state! Me uncle's going to do me room out for me, he's a decorator. And me Nan's give me some money to buy curtains. I've got me sisters suite, their having a new one, it's old like but it's O.K. It'll be a few weeks yet, I'm still cleaning it."

Not all families are as supportive. Some mothers are under pressure to move as soon as the tenancy is accepted, regardless of the condition of the property. Many young women are desparate to move out of hostels. Other women feel it is important to occupy the property as quickly as possible for security reasons, especially in areas of high crime.

"... disgusting! It were a right bloody mess. The wallpaper were hanging off and the doors were all smashed. And it were filthy, really filthy ... I had to stay there, they'd (vandals) have been in, in no time, if I'd left it empty

like. But you couldn't put a bairn in it, he [son] stayed with me Mam for two weeks."

"It were damp and there was cockroaches. It was disgusting. I told them but they just said, 'you accepted it' Honest, it weren't fit for a dog, let alone a bairn. And all round the windows was rotten so the rain came in."

There were similar stories in other areas, with damp, condensation and the general shabbiness of the properties causing the greatest concern. Noticeably, mothers in Blyth Valley and their support workers, such as health visitors, had fewer complaints about the condition of property, which in general was felt to be of a good standard.

Internal decor

All three local authorities offered compensation for poor decorative order, in the form of rent-free weeks. Those who have their rent paid directly to the local authority by housing benefit receive a cheque from the local authority. The city of Newcastle offers a maximum of eight weeks compensation, which, although it may not cover the cost of redecorating a whole house, does compare favourably with local authority compensation in other parts of the country.

Property repairs

The length of time a mother could expect to wait for repairs varied from one authority to another, but does seem to have improved over recent years. In general, the mothers had few complaints about the time taken to get small repairs done, a couple of weeks seeming reasonable to most of them. However, even so-called minor repairs can be important – a missing or broken lock or catch on a cupboard might put a child in danger if it is the only place to keep dangerous domestic substances such as bleach. Although this type of repair might be considered the tenant's responsibility, some mothers have difficulty performing such minor home maintenance without adequate tools. Furthermore, the cost of even the smallest items can be prohibitive to those on income support. To spend £2 or £3 on a cupboard lock will put a strain on the budget for days or weeks. More major repairs, however, did cause concern, with fences and gates being the highest priority in the mother's eyes. One mother in Castle Morpeth reported waiting eight months for a fence to be repaired, during which time she could not let her child play in the garden unsupervised.

Satisfaction with the area

Amongst the mothers themselves and those who work with them, the condition of the first property caused considerably less concern than the area it was in. The young mothers had very sound reasons for wanting to be housed in a particular area. They ranged from a need for parental support, to a need to be housed as far from an ex-boyfriend as possible to avoid harassment. Most mothers were acutely aware of the problems experienced on certain estates, and believed, as did many health visitors, that they were being clustered in the less desirable areas.

Of the 31 mothers living in their own homes, 12 said they did not feel the area they lived in was a good one in which to raise a child. The reasons given related to crime, vandalism, drugs and the behaviour of neighbours and their children:

*"They said I could have a house down the bottom end (of the estate). It was next to the **** [a family known locally for their criminal activity]. I wasn't going to bring up a bairn down there not next to them like! I had to go back to my mam's and wait. Took two years."*

Desire for a particular area was the main reason mothers experienced delay in being housed. Many were aware that they could have a property quickly if they accepted a flat on one of the larger estates or on specific streets within an estate. The delay was in holding out for the property or area of their choice. In most cases, a compromise had to be reached between desire and urgency.

Facilities

Mothers initially felt that their access to facilities was reasonable, most living within walking distance of shops or a post office. However, those living on estates agreed they were restricted to smaller local retailers with inflated prices, or to the use of mobile grocery vans which tour the estates. It is a costly and time consuming journey to the centre of Newcastle from almost all of the city's peripheral estates, and many mothers reported seldom leaving the immediate area they lived in.

Whilst most mothers in the urban areas had easy access to a baby clinic, the same could not be said for the outlying districts within Castle Morpeth and Blyth Valley. Here health visitors had to put on extra clinics to ensure mothers took their babies regularly, as transport in some of the rural areas is restrictive, and even with the additional clinics access was difficult for some. In the city, access to doctors can be a problem, especially for a mother with a young baby. One estate, Cowgate, is served by no less than 37 practices, but not one is actually on the estate itself. In some cases mothers had to make a journey of several miles to reach a doctor. Similarly, pharmacies are, for security reasons, seldom found in the heart of the estates.

A 1984 study set in Glasgow noted that the layout of shops and other facilities on peripheral estates does little to assist a young mother who must make most of her journeys on foot, having little money for bus fares and being encumbered with small children and push-chairs.[8]

Access to family support

Family support is of paramount importance in the early months of independence, and is the main reason for a mother requesting a specific area, even street in some cases. Of the 31 mothers living independently, eight reported having to make a short bus journey (up to 50 pence one way) to visit their families, and a further seven had to make longer and more expensive journeys; 16 were only a short walk away.

It is seldom the case that mothers, even those housed quickly via the homeless route, are placed on the opposite side of the city to their families, as in all areas there are pockets of accommodation with high turn over. Nevertheless, several women felt that poor access to their family in the very early days caused such strain as to tempt them to return home where possible. Some mothers spent a considerable amount of time at their parents' home during the first year of independence, using their own homes simply to sleep in.

Perceptions of policy

"Why do they put us all here? They think it don't matter ... just 'cause we're young. They don't treat you like proper families, just bung us down here. No one wants to live down here."

This mother's comments echo the beliefs of the Housing Services Advisory Group of the DOE when it reported in 1974 that: 'There is a tendency for one-parent families not to be regarded as 'real' families and for local authorities to allocate housing to them on a different basis than that which would apply to a two-parent family'.[9]

Finer, referring to local authority housing in the same year, noted: "Our evidence suggests that unmarried mothers suffer particular discrimination from local authorities in some areas".[10]

In an attempt to identify whether young unmarried mothers suffer discrimination from Newcastle's housing department, this study called upon the assistance of Newcastle's housing needs department, who collect data relating to the desires and outcomes of housing applications.

It should be noted that throughout the study it proved difficult to isolate data or statistics relating solely to single, never-married mothers, and in this case data relates to all lone parents.

Data collected by the housing needs department relates to the 'first choice' location as entered on a housing application form and compares this with the eventual destination of the applicant.

It would be reasonable to assume that if young unmarried mothers, or in this case lone parents in general, were being discriminated against, there would be a discrepancy between their first-choice location and the area they were eventually housed in.

The study compared the data for 1,337 lone parent families and 1,503 two parent families housed in the first six months of 1994. As Figure 2 shows (opposite), there is a general tendency for lone parents to be slightly less likely to get the area of their first choice. This holds true whether the area of first choice is one of the more or less desirable areas in the city.

There are, however, noticeable exceptions. Four areas, Shieldfield (6), North and South Benwell (21 and 24) and Cruddas Park (10), are all more likely to be successful first-choice areas for lone parents. With the exception of Shieldfield, these are recognised as being areas of high crime and social problems. Furthermore, one of the areas least likely to be a successful first choice for lone parents is Gosforth (8), an area considered to be particularly desirable, and resulting in much of the property having been lost to social/public housing through 'Right to Buy'.

This data should not be considered conclusive, however, as many factors other than the composition of the household, or area of first choice, will have an effect on where a family is ultimately housed. For example, the remaining property in Gosforth is predominantly larger, three-bedroomed houses, whereas the property in Shieldfield is predominantly two-bedroom flats, and may be considered by officers to be more suitable for a lone parent.

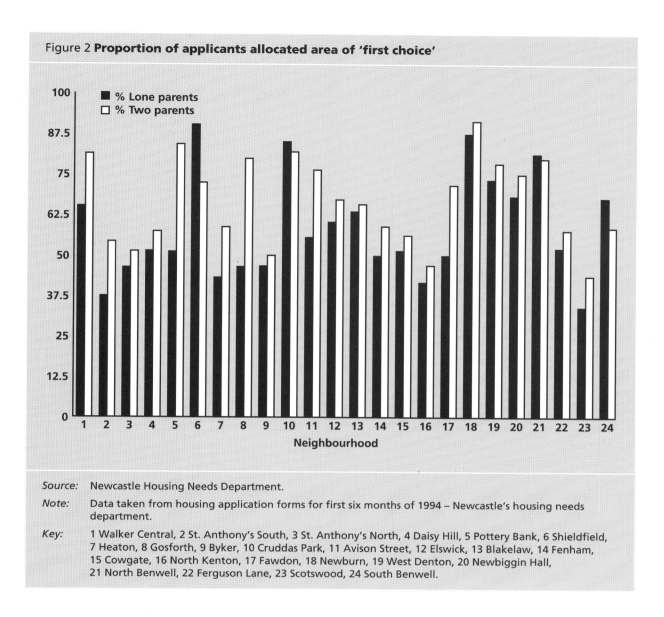

Figure 2 **Proportion of applicants allocated area of 'first choice'**

- ■ % Lone parents
- □ % Two parents

Neighbourhood

Source: Newcastle Housing Needs Department.

Note: Data taken from housing application forms for first six months of 1994 – Newcastle's housing needs department.

Key: 1 Walker Central, 2 St. Anthony's South, 3 St. Anthony's North, 4 Daisy Hill, 5 Pottery Bank, 6 Shieldfield, 7 Heaton, 8 Gosforth, 9 Byker, 10 Cruddas Park, 11 Avison Street, 12 Elswick, 13 Blakelaw, 14 Fenham, 15 Cowgate, 16 North Kenton, 17 Fawdon, 18 Newburn, 19 West Denton, 20 Newbiggin Hall, 21 North Benwell, 22 Ferguson Lane, 23 Scotswood, 24 South Benwell.

Ultimately this study could uncover no evidence to prove or disprove the belief that young mothers are discriminated against by housing officers in Newcastle, or more generally by policy. However, the data do suggest that this could be an area for further research.

What can be said with some certainty is that, both in Newcastle and in the other areas, young mothers do tend to end up in less desirable districts, and in shabbier housing. This is the belief both of mothers and of many of those working with them, and is supported by data held by Newcastle's housing needs department relating to the condition of housing when it is let. However, this may be due to the urgency of their situation, rather than any determined effort on the part of the housing office to discriminate against them. In addition, with much of the better stock in desirable areas lost through 'Right to Buy', what remains, and what is likely to become available, is poorer quality housing on large estates.

Young women's perceptions are to an extent also coloured by their lack of understanding of housing policy and experience of housing in general. Many young mothers have unrealistic notions of what housing is available. A mother brought up in local authority housing all her life, in a more desirable area, may understandably want to remain in that area and live near her parents. What she may not be aware of is the slow turnover of housing in that neighbourhood. The housing officer's encouragement to apply for or accept property in a different area is most often a response to a lack of housing, and the mother's desire to be housed quickly, rather than any intention to discriminate.

It should be noted, however, that if the reports of some mothers are to be accepted, then there are certainly some housing officers in the region with a less than sympathetic attitude to young single mothers. Insults and verbal abuse on both sides are common.

Local authority as enablers

In general, despite the local authority being the first, and in most cases the only, agency a young single mother turns to for housing, what they offer is often less than satisfactory in the mother's own eyes. Nor can they be seen as providing satisfactory advice and support to a young single mother in search of housing, whether or not she is homeless:

"All they [local housing office] did was send me to an advice centre. They weren't much help, gave a list of private landlords and emergency accommodation. Just left me to find a place on my own. They were no help really."

Many of the mothers held a dim view of housing officials. Asked who had been the least helpful person or agency during the time they were trying to set up a home, the answer was often the housing department. On several occasions mothers reported hostility, even verbal abuse, from particular housing officers. It is the government's intention that local authorities should develop more as enablers rather than as providers of housing over coming years and that there be greater use of advice agencies. If this is to be the case, there will need to be much greater liaison and cooperation between housing offices, private landlords and voluntary advice agencies.

Housing associations

The region of the study benefits from the activity of several well established housing associations, with large stockholdings by the largest national housing associations Home Housing Association and North British. There are also a number of smaller, more specialist housing associations such as Newcastle and Whitley Housing Trust. They operate allocation policies based on waiting lists with points systems and their allocation of properties is directed generally towards those who are inadequately housed. As is common practice, it is expected that 50 per cent of their lettings should be to local authority nominations. One housing association, Newcastle and Whitley Housing Trust, has recently closed its waiting list for all properties except for those in three of the less desirable and most difficult to manage areas of the city. It now only deals with local authority nominations or referrals from other recognised agencies for properties in other areas.

Housing association property is generally accepted to be of a better standard and condition than local authority property, and also tends to be spread more evenly across the area rather than being clustered in large estates. This belief is supported by the findings of the English House Condition Survey 1991, which showed housing associations to have the highest percentage of dwellings in best condition, which no doubt reflects the number of new and refurbished dwellings in this sector. Despite this fact, only a little over six per cent of all lone parents in Newcastle live in housing association property.[11] Although housing associations keep a keen eye on housing benefit levels, their assured rents and rents in New Build schemes can be somewhat higher than local authority rents. However, this difference, in many cases, is still covered by housing benefit, and would not cause a problem to a young single mother living on income support.

It is interesting, then, to note that very few mothers had even applied to housing associations, and fewer still lived in housing association property. Only 14 out of the 31 independent mothers had applied. Only two had done so without encouragement; the other 12 had not considered it until it was suggested to them, either by the local housing officer or another advice body. Research by the DOE shows that only 21 per cent of local authority applicants recall being asked whether they wished to be nominated to a housing association.[12] This is reflected by the comments of the mothers, many having no recollection of being asked about nominations. Local housing department officials report a reluctance on the part of some applicants to accept housing association property when it is offered. There are various suggestions as to why this might be, but the most likely reasons seem to be suspicion that a housing association tenancy is less secure than a local authority one, and issues related to cost. Higher rents may not be a problem as long as the tenant is in receipt of full housing benefit. However, if, at a later date, a tenant should escape the benefits trap by working, as many young mothers fully intend to do, they may well lose entitlement to housing benefit, leaving them with unaffordable rent.

There are housing associations and trusts in the region which cater specifically for single people under pensionable age, notably Nomad Housing Group. Young single mothers, however, do not qualify for this accommodation as, although they are single, they require more than a single person's accommodation. Some people experience difficulties if they become pregnant while living in single persons accommodation, as it is clearly not designed for a mother and baby. In such cases the associations can only act as advocates on the expectant mother's behalf, in an attempt to secure her other accommodation, as no associations have yet developed specific accommodation to cover the changing needs of such young women.

Only two associations in the region have schemes specifically for lone parents: Nomad has a small scheme in Bedlington, and New Hope Co-op, a small scheme in Newcastle. Both have very few properties in these schemes, long waiting lists and slow turnover.

Only three of the sample mothers lived in housing association properties at the time of interview. They were all very satisfied with their housing, two having had a succession of local authority properties previously. The third was the only mother in the sample who had a housing association property as her first home.

Private rented housing

During the 1970s both the Finer Committee and the Housing Services Advisory Group expressed concern about the concentration of lone parent families in private rented property, especially furnished accommodation. They feared that this made them vulnerable to decreasing availability, high rents and poor conditions. However, the private rented sector is now expected to play an increasing part in the provision of housing over the coming years. Central to the Government's thinking on housing is the belief that people 'should endeavour to meet their own needs',[13] rather than expecting the state to provide housing for them. Faced with long waits for local authority or housing association property, a number of young single mothers do endeavour to meet their own needs and try to secure private rented accommodation.

Access to private sector

The availability of private rented property differs widely between areas. Castle Morpeth has a very limited private sector, as does Blyth Valley, where it is contained within the main towns. Newcastle has a well developed private sector. However much of this is not available to young single mothers for a number of reasons, and the property which is available is often of a poor standard.

Landlords can command higher rents for a property split into several student units than they can by letting a property whole as 'family'

accommodation. With a high number of students in the area, there would seem to have been considerable development of this nature in recent years.

Landlords who do have family accommodation to let fall broadly into two categories. First, there are the professional landlords and developers whose property is often of a better standard, but also more expensive. A bond and several weeks rent in advance are usually required; even if the weekly rent is affordable in terms of housing benefit, bonds and advance rents can amount to £450 or more. Although housing benefit will pay rent in advance in some cases, it will not cover a deposit, although, in extreme cases, social services will. Many landlords and letting agents will not accept tenants on housing benefit or income support, due as much to the difficulties landlords have with the housing benefit departments as to any concern over the tenants willingness to pay. Housing benefit is notoriously slow, both to initiate and to alter when rent increases are negotiated, or a tenant's circumstances alter. Some housing benefit departments in the region are currently several months in arrears with rent increases. Even for new claimants, it can take several weeks to process a claim and make the first payment. Few young single mothers have money saved up to cover this and few landlords are willing to wait. If the more reliable private landlords are to play a part in housing young single mothers and others on lower incomes, they will require a much more efficient housing benefit system.

In contrast to these professional landlords there are the smaller property developers, small scale property owners and those letting individual properties until they can sell. Many of these are more amenable to housing benefit claimants and may require only one week's rent in advance. For this reason alone, they are more likely to attract young single mothers wishing to move quickly. However they can be somewhat less than reliable when it come to spending money on repairs and safety and providing documentation, many offering no official tenancy agreement. When asked how safe her tenancy was, one mother in a private rented flat in Newcastle reported:

"[He] just said as long as I paid the rent and didn't make any trouble, we could stay, didn't have to sign anything, no."

This hardly offers the security a mother needs.

Similarly, the condition of much of the private rented property in some areas of the city is far from suitable for a young family. This has been demonstrated in a survey by Newcastle's Engineering, Environment and Protection department in 1992, reinforced by the findings of the English House Conditions Survey (1991). One of the areas covered by the Newcastle survey was Scotswood Village, a sub area of the larger Scotswood, where 450 dwellings were subject to a full inspection, 196 (44 per cent) proved to be unfit for human habitation, and 434 properties (96 per cent) were in a poor enough condition to be eligible for a discretionary improvement grant. A similar picture could be seen in Benwell, where 25 per cent of dwellings inspected were unfit for human habitation and 88 per cent below discretionary grant level.

Mothers in private property

Only three of the Newcastle study mothers were living in private rented property; none of the mothers from the other two areas were. These three mothers all resorted to renting from private landlords, having been told that they faced a wait of several years for council property in their chosen areas. In two cases the property was in poor condition, damp and lacking in amenities. In one case, the mother slept in the living room in order that her two year old son could have the only bedroom. One flat was over a betting shop, and access was via the betting shop front door. All three women still had their names on the council waiting list after two years. One of the women had lived in a succession of private flats since leaving a council property she shared with her boyfriend prior to the birth of her baby. Although her flats had been in one of the more sought-after areas of the city, their condition had been less than satisfactory:

"It wasn't really habitable, even the environmental health officer came to see it but he couldn't do anything. It wasn't damp, it was wet, the walls were really wet. It didn't have a kitchen, just some taps and a sink."

In order to find another, more suitable property, she had moved five miles away. She was now living in a better flat, but it was a long way from her friends and family and still had no safe play space for her child. The local authority could give her no hope of a council property back in her own town, as she was, as far as they were concerned, adequately housed.

Satisfaction with a first home

Regardless of the landlord, mothers expressed differing degrees of satisfaction with their housing. 13 were very satisfied, including the three who lived in housing association property, seven were reasonably satisfied, eight were not very satisfied and three, including two in private rented property, were very dissatisfied. Asked what they would most like to change, common answers were the area, the neighbours and the garden or outside play area.

Few mothers had complaints about the type of property. Seventeen lived in houses and 14 lived in flats. Only two expressed any great desire to move from a flat to a house. None of the sample lived in high-rise blocks. In 1993 there were only 80 families with children in Newcastle living in high-rise accommodation and few of these were lone parent families. However, one mother had been given a first tenancy in a tower block on the fifth floor, several years earlier. She had since applied to be rehoused and now lived in a house.

The one mother who owned her own home, which had been bought with money left to her by her father, was very satisfied with her housing. However, she felt that she was trapped to a certain extent as she would never be able to earn enough to take on a mortgage and would therefore never be able to improve on her current situation, especially as the house was unlikely to increase in value greatly.

Furnishing and equipping a first home

3

The vast majority of young women setting up home as single mothers, have never had a home of their own before, unlike many divorced or separated lone parents. They do not own furniture, bedding, kitchen-ware or any of the basics for family life. Although some are lucky enough to have supportive, helpful families, who rally round when housing is eventually found, this is by no means the case for all. Even when a mother's family is supportive, there is often little they can offer in terms of financial assistance or even in the way of furniture or household belongings, many families being stretched to the limit themselves. Furthermore, a young single woman with a child, setting up home alone, does not engender the same spirit of celebration and gift-giving as does a couple setting up home when they marry; they might expect to receive some of the smaller household items, such as towels, crockery or bedding as presents. Many young single mothers need to move into their homes quickly once a tenancy has been accepted and it is rare for them to have acquired much in the way of furniture or equipment. Those who have items offered may have to decline because of lack of storage space. This all results in many mothers having to furnish and equip a home for a young family very quickly and with little money.

Furnished accommodation

Furnished accommodation would be one obvious solution to the problem. However, despite the increase in local authority furnished lettings, especially in Newcastle, few of the sample mothers were aware of this option, and only one had taken it up. Newcastle Metropolitan Borough Council currently has 1,300 furnished tenancies, with one in six new tenancies during the year 1993/4 beginning as furnished, with demand increasing dramatically. The increased rent of approximately £8.50 on a typical furnished tenancy is met by housing benefit for those who qualify. Despite the authorities commitment to furnished accommodation, with a target of 2,500 furnished units by the end of 1994/5, and the very

high take-up rate, it is possible that the message is not being passed to young single mothers in some neighbourhoods, and it is certainly not being targeted at them directly. The majority said they did not know it was available and it had not been mentioned by housing officials. Few professionals and advocates not directly involved in housing knew about this option either.

Those mothers who did know about furnished lettings were put off in some cases by the idea that they would be tied to the furniture for the length of the tenancy. Like any new householder, the mothers wanted to collect together their own belongings and be able to change styles as time progressed and income improved.

Doing without

If furnishings must be bought or borrowed, what standard can mothers achieve in the early months of independence, and how? Mothers living independently were asked to consider a list of basic furniture and indicate which items they did not possess at the time they moved into their first independent home. They were then asked to reconsider the same list, indicating which items they did not have at the point of interview, recalling, if possible, how they had built up the contents of their home and the cost (Table 1, overleaf). The average length of time between the mothers living independently and their interview was 17 months.

The list included only those items which could be said to be essential to daily living and the raising of small children, and was in line with the low cost budget suggested by Bradshaw in his survey on household budgets and living standard.[14] There was one noticeable addition to the list which did not appear in Bradshaw's low cost budget, that of a telephone. It was felt reasonable to include a telephone as essential for young mothers with small children living alone.

It is apparent from the mothers' comments and reports from support and health workers that mothers frequently move into their first homes without the most essential items. This is more

Table 1 **Mothers without basic furniture and equipment**		
	At interview	**On moving in**
Bed (self)	1	7
Bed/cot (child)	1	5
Sofa/Chairs	1	14
Table	16	27
Cooker	0	4
Fridge	8	17
Washing machine	10	21
Dryer	22	25
TV	2	6
Phone	23	26
Carpets (bedrooms)	8	22
Carpets (living room)	1	9
Vacuum cleaner	1	11
N	31	31

Source: *The Newcastle Study,* 1994.

likely for a young woman moving from temporary accommodation, especially if she has little or no family support. Of the mothers in the study, over 50 per cent moved into their homes without at least half of the first 10 items on the list, including seven who moved in without a bed to sleep in and four without a cooker. It is notable that 26 mothers did not have a telephone when they first moved into their homes, and by the point of interview 23 still had no phone.

These findings are backed by the findings of two reports cited by Oppenheim in Pov*erty: The Facts.*[15] The reports, 'Evaluating the Social Fund' and 'Hardship Britain', both outlined the difficulties faced by those on low incomes in providing basic household amenities. They identified beds, cots, bedding and flooring along with washing machines as particular problems.

At the time of interview, few mothers were without the most basic items. All except two had sufficient beds for themselves and their children, all but one had chairs or sofas, and all but two had a television, although the condition was often reported to be poor. All had cookers, although one mother had been without any form of cooker for several months, since she had been broken into and all her belongings stolen. She had only just replaced it.

The majority, 21 of the 31 independent mothers, had a washing machine, and 23 had a refrigerator but only 9 had a dryer. Without a

tumble dryer or very good spin dryer, laundry has to be dried in the house for many months of the year, indeed all year where there is no outside drying area. Launderettes are expensive and often difficult to get to. Drying clothes on radiators and round fires is not only dangerous but causes condensation problems, especially where it is not possible to keep the house at a reasonably high temperature. This is no doubt one of the reasons why so many young women reported 'damp' homes.

Even after several months or years, many mothers still had not managed to carpet some rooms in their homes; eight were without bedroom carpets at the time of interview. Second-hand carpets are difficult to get and usually in very poor condition. Even with the poorest quality new carpet, it will cost upwards of £50 to carpet a typical lounge. Dining tables and chairs were also missing in many cases, but this was due often to a lack of space. In general, by the end of the first 12 months of independence, few were lacking the most basic items. However, the quality and condition was often poor.

Beg, borrow, buy

Mothers could remember quite clearly how they had acquired the furniture they owned by the end of the first year. Some had received social fund loans or community care grants to assist in the purchase of furniture, others had not. Those who had were able to purchase at least some items new. Others bought most, if not all, of their furniture and equipment second-hand.

Referring to the death of an elderly neighbour of her mother's, one young woman commented:

"It's awful really ... but if he hadn't died I'd have nothing. They turned me down for a loan but I used my maternity grant, you know, the £100 they give you. Gave them that for a washer, cooker and the fridge. Then my Mam's friend died and I bought her suite for £50. It's awful really isn't it."

Whilst most accepted that, under the circumstances, they could not expect better, they found genuine problems attached to starting out with second-hand furniture and equipment. The growing trend for old and 'antique' furniture and stripped pine has meant that any items of a decent quality now command a higher price in the junk shops and flea markets than mothers can pay. What remains affordable in the second-hand shops is often the cheaper mass-produced items in poor condition, having served one family

Young Single Mothers: Barriers to Independent Living

already. The life expectancy of such furniture is not long, especially when the demands of small children are put on it. Although mothers had the basics, they frequently reported broken chairs, beds or sofas without springs, and, more alarmingly, faulty electrical goods.

Recent safety legislation relating to the sale of furniture and electrical items, whilst obviously justified, has seriously limited the number of such items on the market and inflated the price of those available. Not all retailers of second-hand electrical goods stick strictly to the law, and there have been prosecutions in the region for the sale of faulty goods.

The real cost of setting up home

The comparative prices of basic furniture and equipment bought new, second-hand or out of a catalogue are shown in Table 2. New prices were taken from local retailers, rather than national stores. Although this means that the prices may not be relevant in all areas of the country, they represent more accurately the goods and prices relevant to the mothers in this study. Catalogue prices were from a well-known home shopping catalogue, and one used regularly by the sample mothers, and were for the cheapest item in each category. Second-hand equipment prices are representative of typical prices for goods in reasonable condition. In the case of electrical goods, items were chosen from dealers who offered at least six months warranty; cheaper

goods were available without warranty. In all cases, the items priced were of basic quality, and typical, in terms of quality and style, of those bought by the sample mothers.

Buy now, pay later

The temptation to buy from home shopping catalogues is great when it can provide essential items quickly for what appear at the time to be small weekly payments. However, even these relatively low weekly payments cause difficulty when the mother's income is so small. The larger items such as a washing machine or cooker are paid for over 100 weeks. Two years is a long commitment for someone whose finances are unlikely to improve. Many young mothers had used catalogues for washing machines, refrigerators and most often baby equipment such as buggies. Like any new mother, the young women naturally wanted the best for their babies and most would rather go into debt than have second-hand cots and buggies. Self-esteem and peer pressure are highly influential factors, and mothers fear they will be judged as bad mothers if they do not. In other cases, the mothers' own parents took out loans or credit in order to buy items for the new home. Where furniture could not be purchased, it was occasionally borrowed. However, most mothers reported that their own families were not in a position to lend much in the way of furniture, especially when there were still siblings at home.

Table 2 **Comparative costs of furniture and equipment**

Item	New £	Second-hand £	Catalogue £	Per week £
Sofa/Chair	199.00	45.00	480.00	6.15
TV	175.00	70.00	239.99	2.95
Table and chairs	60.00	45.00	199.99	5.25
Cooker	239.00	130.00	279.99	3.45
Fridge	139.00	80.00	189.99	2.35
Washing machine	269.00	140.00	279.99	3.45
Dryer	119.00	45.00	129.99	3.40
Double bed	99.00	60.00	149.99	1.85
Single bed	79.00	25.00	84.99	2.25
Carpet 16sq yds	48.00	****	60.00	3.00

Note: Catalogue prices are spread over 20 to 100 weeks
Source: Newcastle Shops and Catalogues, 1994.

It is often the smaller items of household equipment, rather than furniture, which prove most difficult to acquire. Towels, bedding and kitchen-ware are all vital to setting up a home, and are the items least likely to be offered as hand outs by family or friends. They cannot easily be bought second-hand, nor should they have to be. Several mothers reported having insufficient bedding and towels, putting those they did have under great strain:

"Oh sheets me! ... I'd love another pair of sheets, that'd be best. I've only got the one pair so when I wash them I have to get them dry right that day. Usually I can hang them on my Mam's line but sometimes if it rains I have to iron them dry."

"You just don't realise all the stuff you have to get, I never though about a can opener till I'd done my shopping. Couldn't get into the cans could I. Had to keep borrowing my mate's till I could buy one. It's all that stuff you don't think of how much it will all cost do you?"

Acquiring items of this type or extending a stock of bedding usually means resorting to catalogues or credit drapers. The cost of buying these items when initially setting up a home is often underestimated. Table 3 details the cost of the most basic household utilities in two qualities. Prices were taken from stores with national pricing policies. The majority of young mothers will need to make a compromise between price and quality when buying such items. The quality and life span of the basic items is very limited.

Table 3 **Comparative cost of basic household utilities**

16 piece crockery set

16 piece cutlery set

Tin opener

3 pans

Kitchen utensils

Vegetable knife

Oven dishes/bowls

Sheets/pillow cases

Duvet and cover

Pillows (for 1 double bed)

4 hand towels

2 bath towels

Bucket and mop

Sweeping brush

Hand brush and dust pan

Iron and Ironing board

Washing line and pegs

To provide items on this list

Basic Quality £102.00

Standard Quality £166.00

Note: Prices taken from Woolworths and Poundstretcher.

Sources of income and finance

Employment

The mothers in the study had little in the way of employment experience, as might be expected given their young age. Three were working at the point of interview but only part time. However, 22 of the 40 had worked prior to motherhood, doing a range of jobs from bar person to civil servant. They gave up work in order to have and care for their babies. Their reasons for not returning to work were varied, ranging from a very strong belief that it was best for their child, to a lack of maternity rights in employment in many cases, and, most of all, to a lack of child care. Those who were working for some part of their pregnancies were not noticeably better off than those who were on Youth Training placements, or those who had slipped through the net altogether and were unemployed, possibly receiving no benefit at all. The younger working women, especially, had very low earnings and, in general, had not been in the same employment for long enough to qualify for maternity pay and leave. Only a few said that they had been able to save up during the final months of employment and thus prepare financially for the birth.

Prior to the eleventh week before the confinement, a young woman is expected to be on a Youth Training Placement, or in employment. However, an increasing proportion of 16 and 17 year olds are neither in training, education or employment. This proportion is estimated at over five per cent nationally. A report by NACRO, however, indicates that it may be as high as nine per cent in some parts of Tyneside.[16] The report was based on an initiative, which contacted young people in Tyneside who were not in employment or training. Of the 209 teenagers contacted, 62 were young women, of whom 10 were pregnant. The situation for these 10 young women and others like them is very difficult. Unemployed 16 and 17 year olds no longer qualify automatically for benefit, unless they take part in Youth Training schemes. Pregnancy does not make a young woman incapable of working, yet it is very difficult to find employers who are willing to offer placements to young women who will be requiring maternity leave.

The women may under some circumstances qualify for a severe hardship payment if they can prove they are actively seeking employment or are incapable of work. However, severe hardship payments are discretionary, and a mother living at home with her parents may not receive anything.

Income

Income support was the main source of income for the mothers in the study during their pregnancies and as they were trying to set up their homes. It remained so long after they began living independently. None of the sample reported receiving any money from the father of the baby towards preparing for its birth or towards setting up a home. Income support is not payable to a single, pregnant, 16 or 17 year old woman until 11 weeks before the expected date of her confinement, unless she can be shown to be unfit for work. After that time, up to the birth of her baby, she will receive £24.45 between the ages of 16 and 18, if she lives with her parents, and £34.80 in exceptional circumstances, if she lives apart from her family (i.e. for a good reason). After the age of 18 a single pregnant woman will receive £44 per week, regardless of her situation.

Once the baby is born, income support is paid at a higher rate, increased by the dependent child allowance and family lone parent premium. At 16 and 17 years a mother living at home with her parents will receive £56.05 per week, or £64.40 per week if she has 'good reason' to live apart from her family. After age 18 she will receive £73.60 per week whether at home or alone.

Providing for the new arrival

All mothers on income support receive a maternity grant of £100 to assist with the purchase of baby equipment. However, as Table 4 shows (overleaf), the cost of providing even the most basic of equipment for a new baby is far in excess of this.

Table 4 Cost of basic baby equipment

Item	Basic Quality £	Standard Quality £	Catalogue £	Per week £
Cot	80.00	164.00	99.99	3.10
Carry cot/ push chair	189.00	268.00	245.00	2.45
Standard buggy	39.99	119.00	29.99	1.50
High chair	39.99	60.00	29.99	1.50
Cot linen	64.00	80.00	66.00	3.30
Bottles and steriliser	14.00	17.00	34.99	1.75
Stair gate	22.00	25.00	34.99	1.75

Note: Prices for basic and standard quality are from Mothercare.

Source: Catalogue prices taken from a national home shopping catalogue, 1994.

Under different circumstances, the birth of a new baby is cause for great celebration. Many married mothers can expect to receive numerous gifts of baby clothes, bought or knitted by friends or relatives. The forthcoming birth of an illegitimate child is not viewed with such joy, and its mother, more in need of such gifts, is less likely to receive them. In the words of a young mother in Blyth Valley:

"... I thought it would be right after a while ... they'd get used to the idea, be happy for me but nobody said `Oh that's great' nobody said `congratulations'. Only my Mam, in the end she came round, bought us things for the bairn. You'd have thought some one was dying, not being born."

Table 5 shows the costs of a basic selection of clothes to fit a newborn baby. The items were priced in a local market shop and represent the minimum amount and quality needed to clothe a baby for the first few weeks of life. In no way does the quality or style allow for the natural pleasure and pride a new mother feels in dressing her baby to show him or her off to family and friends. It must be remembered, also, that the purchase of baby clothes is not a one-off event, and the items on the list will have to be replaced many times during the first year as the child grows.

"Our Katrina [sister] gives us some things from her bairn but he's a boy. Well you can't go putting a little girl in lad's gear. I'd love to go to Mothercare and just buy all that lovely stuff you see. She'd [baby daughter] look right good in all that bright coloured stuff and them little dungerees and that. I get a lot from my sister's club for her, it's the only way I can afford."

The high cost of equipment and clothing can leave very little per week for food. In fact there is concern amongst doctors and other health workers about the level of nutrition of young single pregnant women on income support. One of the mothers in the study, who was expecting her first child and living alone, had, after her fuel and other commitments, just £9.00 per week to spend on food. Not surprisingly, her nutrition was minimal, her health was suffering and her health visitor was concerned about the development of her unborn child. Weekly food consisted mainly of bread and soup, or the occasional sandwich at a friends house.

Table 5 The cost of basic baby clothes for new born baby

Vests x 6

Baby grows x 6

Plastic pants x 4

Cardigans x 4

Bonnets x 2

Shawl x 1

Mittens x 2 pairs

Total price £59.00

Source: Prices were taken from typical market shops in Newcastle, 1994.

Social fund

Changes to the social security system in 1988 saw the introduction of the social fund, with its system of loans and grants, as a replacement for the previous single payments. This remains the main source of financial assistance to a young single mother requiring capital to set up home, offering, in theory, interest free loans of between £30 and £1000, and, in extreme cases, grants. However, applications for social fund budgeting loans cannot be made until a mother has been on income support for 26 weeks. Given that most cannot receive income support until 11 weeks before the expected date of confinement, most cannot even apply until the baby is 16 weeks old. This effectively delays the point at which many young single mothers can begin to purchase household and baby equipment.

The social fund is not held in high regard by the mothers themselves, who see social fund officers as guardians of the fiscal purse. In the words of one mother:

"You have to fight for every thing, every single penny, makes you feel like a criminal but what else can you do, where else can you get any money to buy things … it's not as if your not going to pay it back, is it?"

Application failures

There would appear to be considerable inconsistency in the allocation of social fund budgeting loans and grants. They are discretionary and are subject to the interpretation of need by the individual officers processing the application and the amount of money remaining in the budget at the time; refusals are common. Indeed the refusal rate for loans and grants has given cause for concern since the system was introduced. By December 1991, the third year of the current system, the overall refusal rate for grants and loans nationally had risen to 73 per cent and 47 per cent respectively.[17]

Mothers and professional support workers, including welfare rights advisers, are often bemused as to how decisions are made about who gets a loan, who gets a grant and who is refused entirely, with mothers of equal need, and similar circumstances, being treated differently. This is demonstrated by the case of two sisters, one of whom was interviewed as part of the study, who applied for loans for basic furniture to set up home. Their circumstances were virtually identical, each wishing to leave the same family home, for the same reasons. Each had been in receipt of income support for over 12 months and each had a small child and a new council house. Each applied to the same office but in different years and at different times of the year. The older woman received a loan of £750 and the younger woman was refused one entirely.

It is the experience of many mothers and professionals working to support them that a successful application is unlikely without some form of advocacy. Certainly among the mothers in the study, those who applied on their own were in the main unsuccessful. Of the 31 study mothers who had set up an independent home, 18 had applied for a loan and eight were refused.

Too poor for a loan

Some mothers reported being refused a loan on the grounds that they could not afford to repay it. They were not, however, encouraged to apply for a grant in its place. Other mothers, all too aware of their limited income, felt deterred from applying for loans because of the financial strain the repayments would cause, and initially applied for a grant. However, the failure rate for grants, generally given only to prevent individuals being taken into care, is so high that mothers were pressured into applying for loans:

"They [social security officers] said I'd not get a grant, so I didn't waste my time asking just went for a loan. Then if they didn't go and tell me I couldn't afford to pay it back so I couldn't have one. Well that's why I wanted a grant isn't it stupid."

Challenging the decision

Unsatisfactory decisions on loan or grant applications can be taken to review. However, without an advocate, a review is also unlikely to succeed. The tactics of some social fund Officers at review seem harsh. One hostel worker told of a Social Fund Officer refusing to allow a small amount for a wardrobe on the grounds that in the area where the applicant lived 'they keep their clothes in bin liners'. Very few young mothers, with already extremely low self-esteem, have the confidence to challenge the local Social Fund Officers. Ironically, the chances of success are greater at a further review, which is held by a Social Fund Inspector. Having less regard for local budgets and guidance, and giving more time to the review, the Social Fund Inspectors tend to produce a higher standard of decision-making than Social Fund Officers.

A mother who is refused a loan may not reapply for another 26 weeks, except when the refusal was on the grounds that she had not been in receipt of income support for the required period or if there have been significant changes in her circumstances. Thus a mother refused a loan to buy essential furnishings will have to wait six months before reapplying. Refusal can result in mothers borrowing from friends or family in some cases, or seeking other, more expensive forms of credit, such as licensed or unlicensed credit brokers or loan sharks.

Those who were not refused entirely often received less than they applied for. This resulted in them buying second-hand goods rather than new. In some cases these did not last long, leaving the mother without the item and yet still needing to pay off the loan taken to buy it. Second loan applications might be made to replace the item but are seldom successful.

Loan repayments

The weekly repayment of budgeting loans varies depending on the amount borrowed. The Benefits Agency aims to recover the money within 78 weeks, or 104 weeks where there have been additional loans and the original sum increased. Repayments are calculated at 15 per cent of total income support where there are no existing commitments, such as fuel direct, 10 per cent where there commitments of up to £6.60 per week, and 5 per cent when existing commitments exceed £6.60 per week. The maximum repayment is 25 per cent of total income support a week. It is clear, however, that in some areas Social Fund Officers are treating 15 per cent as the recommended rate. In one study, repayment rates of up to 20 per cent were reported.[18]

Repayments are taken directly from income support at source. Whilst this serves to ensure that the agency does recover the loan, it allows no margin for budgeting or dealing with fluctuations in weekly expenditure. The emergence of the social fund, with its propensity to offer loans rather than grants, has put added strain on the already inadequate incomes of many young mothers, turning what was originally a short-term budgeting problem into long-term debt.

Grants

Some young mothers make the transition to independent living from a supported hostel or homeless unit. For these women community care grants may be available from the social fund before the birth of the baby. Six of the study mothers applied for grants; four were successful. All received virtually the amount they applied for, two receiving £1000, one receiving £850 and the fourth £775. Applicants must be in receipt of income support. However, there is no requirement to have been in receipt of income support for 26 weeks as with social fund budgeting loans. Under the guidelines given to Social Fund Officers, community care grants should be available to those re-establishing themselves in the community following a stay in residential care. However, the definition of 'residential care' is sometimes contentious. One mother and baby hostel in Newcastle frequently has its clients turned down for community care grants, as the local Social Fund Officers do not recognise the hostel as a provider of residential care because the mothers look after themselves in the hostel – do their own cooking and washing – and the hostel does not provide 24-hour on-site support. However, it does provide more than just accommodation; support covers such things as budgeting and nutrition training and parent craft. Indeed, the hostel in all respects dedicates itself to preparing young mothers to re-enter the community.

As with budgeting loans, the minimum payment for community care grants is £30. However, there is no longer a legal maximum amount for community care grants. The guidelines suggest that the amount requested should be paid, unless it is unreasonable.

There would seem to be no less controversy surrounding the allocation of community care grants than social fund budgeting loans. Workers in supported hostels in Newcastle report running battles with Social Fund Officers over refusals. However, in nearby Gateshead, hostel workers report good rapport with the social fund office and a high level of success. As with loans, much seems to depend on the available budget at the time and the officer processing the application. Any hostel support worker can list numerous cases of what seem to be unfair decisions.

Support and assistance

5

One frequent complaint voiced by the mothers in the study was that they felt they had little practical support during the time they were trying to set up their first homes. Many did have supportive and helpful families. However, even those parents who were supportive could not always offer informed advice when it came to benefits, housing or loan applications. Most often the mothers were led round the system by other young mothers who had worked it out for themselves previously.

For any young woman who finds herself unexpectedly pregnant and alone, and possibly faced with having to leave her current accommodation, there are immediate questions to be asked. 'Where will I get money from? Where will I live? How will I buy baby equipment and furniture?' There is currently no agency in the region studied which can provide answers to all these questions and offer practical help on issues such as transport, child-care information and counselling, in a manner in which the mothers can accept. Many mothers reported being sent from one agency to the next to get support and help.

Statutory support services

Few young mothers have social workers, unless they have been in care or had social worker support in their own right as a child. A major complaint from all professional fields was that, in some areas, it was virtually impossible to get a social worker involved with a young single mother unless there was proof that her child was in imminent danger. As one health visitor put it:

"Social workers can do nothing other than police child abuse these days. If you can't show them bruises, they don't want to know ... by then the damage is done." (Health Visitor)

Of the five women who did have social workers, few found them reliable or even particularly helpful in real terms when it came to establishing a home. Doubtless, their power as advocates was helpful, when loan applications were made, but in general they could not provide

much in the way of baby equipment, furniture, transport, or regular visits to offer support. It was these more positive and practical things which the majority of mothers needed.

Professionals in other fields, such as housing and health, often do not feel they can rely on social services to provide continued support. One housing welfare officer reported a case in which she reluctantly allocated a property to a 16 year old mother in the local homeless persons unit, on the understanding that there would be regular visits by social services. After the first visit, the social worker went on long-term sick leave, the department was too short-staffed to cover her case load, and the mother had no further visits. Problems developed with boyfriends, all night parties and neighbours' complaints, resulting in the mother leaving her home and moving in with friends, eventually to return to the homeless persons unit some months later. This was exactly the scenario predicted by the housing welfare officer if social services did not provide support.

This lack of communication and cooperation between housing, social services and other statutory support services in many areas leaves young mothers who do get offered a tenancy without any back-up during the initial few weeks, as they try to move in and furnish their properties.

The most helpful

The majority of support and advice seems to come from Health Visitors, many of whom act as welfare rights advisers, advocates, confidants, even chauffeur when necessary. However, this undoubtedly puts a strain on the more specific health-related work of health visitors. Ante-natal clinics in some areas often resemble welfare rights and housing advice sessions.

The least helpful

Least helpful in the eyes of the mothers were housing department and Social Security officers, who were perceived to be trying to prevent mothers from becoming independent, or even to be punishing them for becoming single mothers in the first place. Many mothers found them to be difficult, even rude and offensive in some cases. However, it is only fair to say that the officers themselves held a similar view of many young mothers. Certainly, some housing welfare officers do intervene to ensure that young mothers get reasonable properties and locations. Unfortunately, this often means a longer stay in homeless persons accommodation, especially in more rural areas, waiting for a better property. The mothers often see this as unfair interference.

Youth workers were not thought of by the mothers as particularly helpful. They appeared to be concentrating on youth on the streets, predominantly young men, and only one of the mothers in the study was visited in the first few weeks of independence by a youth worker. In Newcastle, the Single Persons Advice Team offers support and advice to young people, especially those who are homeless. However, their involvement with young mothers seems to be minimal. One young mother in Newcastle was told she could expect a visit by a young persons' support worker as soon as she had moved into her own home. Two months later, she telephoned to see if anyone was going to visit, as she needed help with a loan application. A worker eventually visited some weeks later; by this time the mother had managed the application alone, and did not welcome her delayed support.

Youth work has developed as a predominantly urban practice, concentrating on city centres and disadvantaged inner city areas. The mothers in the peripheral areas, especially in Blyth Valley, had no knowledge of youth workers in their areas.

Voluntary support

Voluntary bodies, such as advice agencies and community development projects, play only a small part in supporting young single mothers. Of the sample of mothers, only three had used any form of agency, such as welfare rights or housing advice agency. There were practical reasons for this in some cases, as often mothers knew of the existence of such support agencies but found it difficult to access them. Not all the mothers had access to telephones, and many of those who did had such low confidence that they found them difficult to use. Lack of funding has meant many advice services now have limited opening hours. The combination of lack of confidence, pregnancy or a small child, little money for bus fares and restricted opening times meant many mothers found the whole

process too difficult and preferred to take the advice of their peers.

There seems to be less knowledge of advice and support agencies in the more rural areas. Only one of the sample mothers from Blyth Valley and Castle Morpeth had sought advice from an agency (the agency, Housing Aid for Youth, has since closed). In Blyth Valley, the voluntary sector has made little headway, and those agencies which do exist are concentrated in the main towns. Many are under threat of closure from lack of funding. In these more rural areas, where young mothers are more isolated and public transport is less accessible, there is a greater need for outreach support to young mothers and other vulnerable members of the community. However, the main focus for the development of voluntary and community services has been on local authority estates in towns and inner cities.

Hostel support

The majority of young mothers in mother and baby hostels are there because they have little or no family support. The professional support offered to those young women was quite intense in some cases. They certainly benefited from well informed hostel workers, who could assist with social fund applications, benefits advice and who knew of good sources of furniture and baby equipment. Even where the hostel workers could not be of direct help, they could act as enablers, steering, and if necessary, taking the mothers to other agencies. It is the accessibility of this support which makes it work. Whilst hostel workers are seldom specialist welfare rights or housing advisers, they are on hand and it requires little effort to access their support.

Where mothers from supported hostels find the greatest difficulty is in making the transition from the hostel to fully independent tenancy in one move, without adequate after-care support. Without exception, the hostel workers who took part in this study felt extreme concern at the level of after care they could provide to young women leaving their hostels. They felt that, without continued support, a high percentage of these young women would fail at first independence.[19]

Conclusions to Part I

6

Despite the fact that most mothers did retain a reasonable relationship and level of contact with their families, the families were able to offer little in the way of practical or financial help or advice. Mothers were left very much on their own to establish their independence, and a number of factors relating to housing and finance could prevent or deter them from doing so. The following sections offer some summary comments on the problems young single mothers encounter in establishing their first home.

Housing

When applying for local authority accommodation, and indicating the neighbourhood of first choice, a mother must make a compromise between her standards and the urgency of her housing need. This fact alone makes many mothers select areas which they are aware of as having social problems or poor quality housing.

Those applying for accommodation via the homeless route will fall into the 'one-offer trap'. Although housed quickly, the property will, by necessity, be in an area of high turnover, and generally difficult to let, yet must be accepted, regardless of the mothers standards, desires and needs.

The study found no evidence to support the mother's belief that they were discriminated against by local authority housing policy or practice and deliberately housed in poorer areas. Whilst this clustering is evident, it stems from the fact that these are the only areas where property is readily available.

Homeless temporary accommodation in the region is generally of a poor standard and detrimental to the well-being of a young mother and child. However, better quality accommodation, with the addition of support facilities as is the case with many mother and baby hostels, could turn what is currently a negative experience of homelessness into a more positive preparation for independence.

The loss of so much property through 'Right to Buy' in some neighbourhoods has resulted in waiting lists of several years for some areas. Such a long wait puts a great strain on families supporting their single daughters and grandchildren while they wait their turn for property, and can result in the breakdown of family relations leading to threats of, or actual, homelessness.

The condition and availability of private sector property, and the limited awareness of housing associations, effectively limits young single mothers to local authority property. There is an urgent need for improved quality of housing advice, not only for young single mothers but for all young people.

Finance

The additional financial burden facing young single mothers building a home from scratch on income support, rather than simply living on it, is not recognised by the existing benefit structure.

The payment of income support at a lower rate to mothers under 18 years puts a further burden on the very young women who must live apart from their families. These very young mothers are the most vulnerable, and least well prepared, having poor budgeting and living skills, yet they receive the least support financially.

The extremely low income support paid to a pregnant young woman under 18 years of age, who is forced to live apart from her family, makes it impossible for her to prepare a home for the arrival of her child. There is major concern amongst health workers for the health of both mother and unborn child, given the poor-quality diet which can be achieved on such a low income. In addition, her financial problems are exacerbated by the income support 26-week qualifying period before she can apply for a loan or grant from the social fund.

There is considerable inconsistency around the allocation of social fund loans and grants. This system is too often failing to assist at all, and, where it does offer assistance, it is too little and too late, forcing mothers into less desirable forms of credit, at the very beginning of their independence.

Furniture and equipment

The lack of furniture and equipment in the early weeks and months of independence is not simply a nuisance, it can produce real hardship and long-term problems. For example, the lack of adequate laundry facilities, resulting in the drying of clothes around fires and radiators, may be the cause of much of the dampness and condensation reported by mothers and may ultimately be linked to a growing number of respiratory problems.

The lack of telephones for both social contact and emergency communication intensifies the feelings of isolation, and compounds practical difficulties for those without access to private transport.

In order to furnish and equip a home to the minimum standard, the mothers had to make a compromise between doing without, having poor quality equipment (which may last only a short time), or going into debt. Although willing to help, most families could offer little in the way of furnishings from the family home.

Despite the major growth in furnished tenancies in Newcastle, few young mothers had any knowledge of this as a means to furnishing their property. There is a need for this accommodation to be targeted at specific groups. All accommodation and support providers in the region recognised the acquisition of decent furnishings as a major problem.

Advice and support

There is no one agency, either statutory or voluntary, which can offer young single pregnant women, or women with children, accurate advice on housing and benefits in an accessible manner. Most mothers gained their knowledge of 'the system' from peers. There is a need for a 'One Stop Shop' of advice for young single mothers. The existing youth advice agencies, such as Street Wise, whilst offering an effective service to many, are not presenting themselves in a manner attractive to young mothers.

There is an urgent need for better liaison between housing, social services, health departments, and voluntary bodies in the region, to provide some form of reliable support to young single mothers, especially those housed in local authority property. This might be undertaken as an extension to the Community Care Programme.

The situation in Castle Morpeth and Blyth Valley was more serious, with very little voluntary sector involvement in these areas. The major housing advice agency for young people in Blyth Valley has recently been forced to close due to lack of funding.

Notes to Part I

1   Skuse, T. (forthcoming) Trust for the Study of Adolescence (Brighton)

2   Department of the Environment (1991). *Housing Statistics.* HMSO (London)

3   Department of the Environment (1994). *Access to Local Authority and Housing Association Tenancies, Consultation Paper.* HMSO (London)

4   Institute of Housing (1993). *One Parent Families – Are They Jumping the Housing Queue,* Briefing Paper Autumn 1993. Chartered Institute of Housing (Coventry)

5   Haskey, J. (1989). 'One Parent Families and their children in Great Britain: numbers and characteristics', *Population Trends No.55.* OPCS (London)

6   National Census data, 1991, OPCS (London)

7   The Children Act 1989, Schedule 13 para 26. HMSO (London)

8   Robertson, I.M.L. (1984). 'Single Parent Lifestyles and Peripheral Estate Residence', *Town Planners Review,* 55 (2)

9   See also Karn, V. and Henderson, J.W. (1987). *Race Class and State Housing: Inequality and the Allocation of Public Housing in Britian.* Gower (London)

10 *The Report of the Committee on One-Parent Families* (The Finer Report) (1974). Vol.1. HMSO (London)

11 National Census Data (1991). OPCS (London)

12 Department of the Environemnt (1994). *Housing Research Summary No. 16.* HMSO (London)

13 Department of the Environment (1994) (note 2)

14 Bradshaw, J. (1993). *Household Budgets and Living Standards.* Joseph Rowntree Foundation (York.)

15 Oppenheim, C. (1993). *Poverty: The Facts* Child Poverty Action Group. pp. 74–5.

16 NACRO (1993). *Youth choices – Improving the Uptake of Training by Unemployed Young People.* National Association for the Care and Resettlement of Offenders (London)

17 Craig, G. (1993). 'Aspects of Credit and Debt', *Classification and Control: The Role of the Social Fund* (Chapter 7). Sweet & Maxwell (London)

18 National Association of Citizens Advice Bureaux (1990). *Hard Times for Social Fund Applicants* National Association of Citizens Advice Bureaux (London); see also Craig (1993) (note 17)

19 Skuse (forthcoming) (note 1)

Part II
Barriers to maintaining independent living

Introduction

7

Having managed to establish a home of her own, a young single mother must learn to live in it as an independent adult. This is not without problems, and it is clear that the lives of many young single mothers are extremely turbulent, especially for the first few years.

Of the 40 mothers in the study, seven had given up their first independent home within the first 12 months. The reasons for this were varied. Two of the women attributed their 'failure' to the factors associated with the actual property. Both found their flats too large and difficult to heat, furnish and decorate:

"... if I could have got it right, like a real home right away. It were clean, my Mam saw to that but I didn't have no curtains, and it were cold and just horrible to be there ... so I asked my Mam could I go back and I think she were glad really ... I don't know what I'd have done if she said 'no'."

Another two returned home because of dissatisfaction with the area, and concerns about the neighbours and crime. One mentioned during her interview that she had fled her home because of domestic violence and another because of threats and harassment from a neighbour: both moved into supported accommodation. Another woman said simply that she found the whole business too difficult:

"It were everything really, the flat, the bairn, money ... Couldn't make ends meet, don't know how anyone can."

Within local authority housing, across all areas of the city, between eight and ten per cent of tenancies terminate within the first few weeks. This figure increases still further to approximately 13 per cent for first-time tenancies. However, there is a noticeable difference when the property is furnished as these tenancies generally last longer. Housing needs workers believe the key factors involved to be poverty and isolation.

All young people leave home at some point and become independent. In some cases, as with students or young people leaving home to share flats with friends or work mates, or even to marry or cohabit prior to having children, there is an apprenticeship period: a time when it is acceptable to return home frequently, to run out of money, when it is not seen as important to have all the material comforts of family life; a time when independence does not require permanent housing, and the setting down of roots. During this period it is legitimate to call the whole thing off and return to the family home. The skills required for independence are developed slowly and the standard of independent living is improved gradually over the years. Problems arise for many young single mothers because this apprenticeship period is not available. They are catapulted into responsible adulthood and motherhood simultaneously, with no practice. They are expected to get it all right immediately, or be seen as bad mothers and failures:

"... because I'm so young I suppose, they look at you like you're a slag, like you can't possibly look after a baby, as if you're going to hurt it or something."

8 A house is not a home

Dissatisfaction with housing

As has been discussed, a young woman with a child being housed via the homeless route is not in a position to be too choosy about the condition or location of her first home. In any case many, unaware of the problems their first homes have, lack the experience to foresee cold winters, damp walls, draughts and large heating bills. They do not recognise potential isolation, nor consider the cost of public transport in order to reach their families, or even a selection of good shops:

"Just if they'd given me a nice little place. It [a privately rented flat] was too big. I couldn't pay the heating and couldn't never have got it nice. Didn't think at the time, I just wanted my own place like."

This mother admitted that she had been overcome with the excitement of having her first home and getting away from her parents. However, the reality had proved too hard and, after incurring fuel and rent debts, she left to spend time living with friends and eventually moved into a mother and baby hostel.

The 'playing house' scenario has a lot to answer for. Just as with older women, many mothers have very vivid images of how they want their homes to be. They are as house-proud as any new householder. Unfortunately, with very limited incomes and little ability to realise their dreams, they often become disillusioned. A young single mother living alone with her baby spends a great deal of time in her home, and something as seemingly trivial as internal decor can be the cause of extreme stress. Staring at drab, tatty and possibly damp walls for many hours of the day is enough to depress anyone, yet decorating, whilst simple enough for many, is a major problem if a mother cannot afford basic tools and step ladders, has no experience and cannot afford even the cheapest paint and paper. At the lowest prices, wood-chip paper and emulsion paint for a typical lounge will cost £30–£40, money which has to be saved out of income support. Advice and volunteer agencies report many requests for free decorating and gardening services. Unfortunately, when community decorating services are set up they tend to be slanted towards non-domestic buildings, such as community centres, nursing homes and hostels.

Although the majority of mothers living in flats, rather than houses, did not express dissatisfaction with the type of housing, they did encounter problems. These were mainly the lack of a garden for the child to play in and nowhere to hang out washing. Surprisingly few complained about access difficulties, with only one of the flat dwellers living above the first floor.

Conversely, those living in houses sometimes expressed concern and difficulty with the garden. Many felt that, at this stage in their lives, it was enough to manage a home and child. A garden, with long grass, weeds, broken fences and gates, was just added burden:

"Oh it were in a right state, there was weeds and rubbish and broken stuff ... fences and that, and no fence at all at the bottom ... bairns could get right out to the road ... What good's that like?"

Few had money to purchase gardening tools and felt that a dangerous garden was little better than no garden. Some mothers had applied to be rehoused in flats as a solution to the problem.

Dissatisfaction with the area

Although the young mothers displayed a remarkable ability to transform an empty house or flat into a furnished home within a few months, they were not able to transform the area. Without doubt, problems with the area were a far greater cause for concern than the property itself, and more likely to cause a mother to seek rehousing or even to return home. Most of the women had very high standards for their children and were concerned with the standards in the environment around them:

"Can't let him play out, not round here, with the swearing and that.'

"They get put here, nice enough lasses but they just get dragged down. You can watch the difference in them over the months."

(Social Worker)

Crime

Others were concerned with the high level of crime in some areas. One mother reported having to get her own mother to sit in the house whilst she went out to the shops. Levels of crime are so high in some areas of Newcastle that contents insurance is either too expensive or not available at any price. One mother of five had been burgled some months prior to the interview and lost virtually everything. Having no insurance and being refused a social fund loan, she was unable to replace her belongings. She had to give up the house, in effect, becoming homeless as a direct result of a burglary, which she believed was committed by her neighbour.

She was offered temporary accommodation in the homeless family's unit. However, that would have necessitated three of her children changing schools. She spent nine months living in overcrowded conditions with her sister on the same estate before she was eventually rehoused by a housing association in the area.

Vandalism and misuse

It was not so much major crime which the majority of mothers complained about, as the level of vandalism, joy-riding, drug-taking and general misuse of the area they encountered. Misuse of common areas is significantly higher within local authority housing than any other tenure.[1] Whilst most mothers felt that they could control and protect their own children while they were at home, they expressed real worries about what would happen when they went to school or began to play with other children in the area:

"He's getting a right little bugger these days ... it's since he started playing out, around. Started answering back and kicking me ... and swearing! He's not heard that from me, not in this house."

"You see them ... [youths] all at the back of the garages at night. They're sniffing like ... and other stuff. They don't even try to hide it, you can see the bags and things in the

morning. The bairns pick stuff up. I've reported it but they didn't do nowt."

The worries of the mothers about the environment generally echoed the findings of a recent report from the Joseph Rowntree Foundation on work by various agencies on difficult-to-manage estates.[2] In the study, estate managers identified problems with high rates of crime and vandalism and high numbers of alienated young people with little prospect of work. In addition, estate managers are aware of the numbers of young children with few facilities.

Rehousing and transfers

Twelve of the sample mothers had applied to be rehoused at some point for a range of reasons including dissatisfaction with the area or property or a need for a larger property to accommodate a second child.

The housing needs of any family change as the children grow, and this is no less true for single-mother families. The needs of a young single woman with her first baby can be very different to her needs a few years later. In the first stages of independence her priority might be family support: in order to remain near her family she may overlook all other factors, such as crime, facilities or type of property. However, as she becomes more established as an independent adult and mother, and her child begins to play outside, requiring playmates, a garden and other facilities, she may become more aware of the quality of the neighbourhood and the suitability of her home and subsequently apply to be rehoused:

"I'm on the list like but I don't know how long it will take. It's shocking round here now. Never used to be like this when I were a kid. It were ok then. I can't take much more, daren't hardly go out of my house."

The housing trap

Rehousing presents far greater problems than initial housing, as, unless a mother is awarded points for harassment, ill health, or serious under- or over-accommodation, she is no longer seen as a priority.

In Castle Morpeth during 1993/4 there was a total of only 240 properties available for re-letting. Priority for these properties naturally goes to those with the most urgent housing need, generally those threatened with homelessness.

Mutual exchanges are encouraged as one solution to the problem, and have increased fourfold in recent years.

In Blyth Valley an added difficulty is that a tenant is required to have been in a property for 12 months before a transfer can be entertained. Here again the shortage of properties means a wait of several years, unless there are exceptional circumstances. The option of taking a property in a less desirable area is not available in Blyth Valley – there is an acute shortage of properties in all parts of Blyth Valley.

The severe shortage of decent housing stock in all areas makes it impossible to develop a flexible allocations policy. Yet a degree of flexibility is required to cater for the changing nature of people's housing needs and desires. The concept of housing 'careers' or 'pathways' to map a changing housing need was the basis for work done by Payne and Payne in 1977.[3] Their study indicated that the movement of a family along its housing pathway was a consequence of its initial housing status at the time of the first pregnancy. A young single mother and her family will develop, no less than any other family, a housing career, as their needs and desires change. Yet with allocations policies based so heavily on spatial requirements, it is difficult to demonstrate need if the family is adequately housed in terms of space. Thus mothers often find themselves in a form of 'housing trap', lured to a property and area by the attraction of speedy housing, then trapped there as they are considered adequately housed unless they require more room.

The greater availability of property in Newcastle does make obtaining rehousing slightly easier but, again, only as long as a mother is realistic in her choice of area and does not apply for housing in areas of slow turnover. Newcastle's housing department reports that the majority of families wish to move less than two miles, most wishing to remain in the same neighbourhood. However, there is a slight difference between two parent and one parent families. As Figure 3 shows, there is a general tendency for lone parents to be less satisfied with

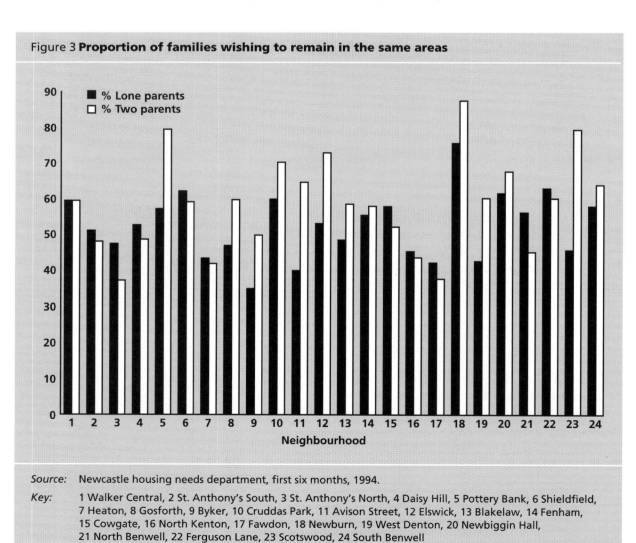

Figure 3 **Proportion of families wishing to remain in the same areas**

■ % Lone parents
□ % Two parents

Neighbourhood

Source: Newcastle housing needs department, first six months, 1994.

Key: 1 Walker Central, 2 St. Anthony's South, 3 St. Anthony's North, 4 Daisy Hill, 5 Pottery Bank, 6 Shieldfield, 7 Heaton, 8 Gosforth, 9 Byker, 10 Cruddas Park, 11 Avison Street, 12 Elswick, 13 Blakelaw, 14 Fenham, 15 Cowgate, 16 North Kenton, 17 Fawdon, 18 Newburn, 19 West Denton, 20 Newbiggin Hall, 21 North Benwell, 22 Ferguson Lane, 23 Scotswood, 24 South Benwell

Young Single Mothers: Barriers to Independent Living

their current neighbourhood and request transfers to different areas.

Of the sample mothers who expressed a desire to move, some wished to move very short distances, to the other end of the same road in some cases, or simply away from a particular family. Others, noticeably those who were not near their families, hoped to move to another neighbourhood. Had they been nearer to the support of their famileis, they may have been better able to cope with the problems they encoutered in the areas where they were housed.

Ill health

Whether a mother's dissatisfaction stems from changing perceptions of an area, the fact that she didn't want to live there in the first place, or problems with the property can have an adverse effect on her health. Being trapped in an area or property which is unsuitable can take its toll, especially if compounded by financial stress that has to be endured alone. *Hardship Britain*[4] reported frequent ill health amongst those living on income support, with 65 per cent of adults and 70 per cent of children in families interviewed suffering a range of problems, including asthma and bronchitis. Of the 574 lone parents who were rehoused in Newcastle in 1993/4, over 10 per cent had medical priority points. The main reasons for their medical priority were depression, stemming from the social problems of the area they were living in, and respiratory problems:

"... can't sleep me. Just keep thinking every little noise they're going to break in. Aint got nowt like, don't know what they'd want to get in here for but I still can't sleep for it. It makes you sick after a while ... worrying and no sleep and the bairns and that."

In addition, when a mother had no ground-level access to her property, carrying children and push chairs up stairs could cause back problems. The mothers themselves seemed acutely aware of the effects their situation had on their health.

Violence and harassment

Other women have to leave their own homes for more serious reasons. Despite the lessening stigma attached to single parenthood now, some mothers, particularly very young ones, do experience discrimination, harassment and even abuse. Two of the mothers in the study reported being victims of harassment by youths and children to the point where they had to leave their homes and return to family and friends. Another mother of a six-month-old baby was threatened with violence by a drug dealer who lived in the same building. She eventually fled the flat and lived with friends for several months before being rehoused in another town by a housing association. Despite the police being involved in the harassment case, the local authority would offer her nothing other than temporary accommodation in the homeless families unit, classing her as intentionally homeless. They would not award her points for harassment until they had received reports from the police. Although problems of this kind can be experienced by many residents, the lack of a partner to provide moral support makes young single mothers feel particularly vulnerable.

In the first half of 1994, there were 61 lone parent families with severe harassment points in Newcastle, a figure considered unrealistically low by the housing department and not a true reflection of the real number of women suffering harassment in the city. Harassment often goes unreported for fear of reprisals and the belief that it will not be taken seriously. One doctor, however, felt it likely that victimisation and harassment were the cause of much of the depression he treated in young single mothers.

Domestic violence seems high amongst very young cohabiting couples.[5] Violence was one of the reasons so few young mothers had any relationship with the father of their child. Of those who had subsequent live-in boyfriends, several had experienced domestic violence, and one had to flee her home and go to a refuge very soon after the baby was born. Refuge workers believe unreported domestic violence to be high amongst young single women, whose low self-esteem often makes them more likely to abandon their independence as an escape from a violent or difficult situation, rather than taking out injunctions and remaining in their own homes.

The second child

The arrival of a second child is another reason which can trigger an application to be rehoused. Of lone parents in general, 44 per cent have more than one child, with an average of 1.4 children per single parent family in 1989 as against 1.8 children per two parent family.[6] Most of the young mothers in the study are housed in properties comprising one double bedroom and one single bedroom.

Most of the mothers in the study had only one child; just seven of the mothers from Newcastle and two from Blyth Valley had more than one child. The Newcastle mothers did not experience any real delay in being rehoused into a larger property, all moving before the second child was 12 months old. The two women from Blyth Valley, however, had longer waits.

The serial transfers

The fear of what will happen to their children as a result of growing up in their current neighbour-hoods in the coming years is great enough to make many mothers apply to be rehoused. When an application for transfer is unlikely to be successful for many years, and the current situation is becoming intolerable, mothers sometimes return to their family homes or a friend's home if they can, re-applying at a later date for a new property. This deliberate forfeiting of one tenancy and applying for another might be seen by some as an attempt to speed up the process of moving into a new home. However, there was nothing to suggest, from the mothers interviewed, that this was the case. They gave up their own homes to get away from an unsatis-factory situation for a time, and to return to the security of the family home in most cases. They did not anticipate being housed any faster but, in their view, the wait would be more bearable.

One mother of two had spent several years returning to her mother's home inbetween independent tenancies rather than put up with unsatisfactory housing conditions. This disruption had continued throughout her children's lives until she was eventually housed in the area of her original choice by a housing association. By this time she had become well known to the local housing department as a difficult tenant:

"They think I'm just being difficult. They all know me down the housing. They just think `Oh ignore her, she's just a stupid cow.' But why should I stay if it's no good for the bairns. They know where I want like, a good area, where it's nice for them. So when they offer me a place, I try it, well that's only right aint it. You don't know if you don't live there, not really."

Young men and housing

Boyfriends, whether the father of the child or children, can cause further problems for young single mothers. Young single men experience extreme difficulty in finding accommodation, so the possibility of moving into a ready-made home can be one of the attractions of a potential girlfriend. In theory, this should mean that if the relationship breaks down the mother's tenancy will not be threatened. However, in practice young single mothers can have trouble getting an ex-boyfriend to move out, and more than one mother who was interviewed discovered that a boyfriend had sold some of her possessions – possessions on which she was still repaying a social fund loan.

Finance

Income

Without doubt, the major problem the mothers felt they experienced in the first years of independence was lack of money. Many of the mothers in the study saw this as a potential barrier to their continued independence in the early months. Most mothers needed considerable support from their families in the early weeks as they developed budgeting skills. Borrowing small amounts from family and friends was common. Where this support was not available, the independence was put under great strain.

Lone parents have long been recognised as one of the most financially disadvantaged groups in society, with average incomes being just 38.2 per cent of that of comparable two parent families in 1993:

"... not being able to sleep ... that's what gets me ... I'm alright during the day, with two of them ... too busy to think about it much ... at night, when they're in bed, you start thinking, how am I going to pay this or that. Then by the time I go to bed I can't sleep ... takes hours sometimes. He [the doctor] gave me some tablets but I daren't take them, couldn't wake up next morning, and I'm scared if I don't hear the bairns in the night. Anyway, I don't need tablets, I need £200."

Income support

With little, in some cases no, work experience to help them gain employment, and with very low maintenance payments, despite the development of the Child Support Agency, young single mothers have little chance of improving their situation and may remain trapped on income support for many years. Mothers of 16 and 17 years, with one child, receive £64.40 per week; from 18 years of age they receive £73.60. This is increased by £15.56 for every child under 11 years of age.

Maintenance

In 1991 Bradshaw and Millar noted that those mothers who were receiving regular maintenance payments were more likely to be working than those who were not.[7] Since 1992, in a move to assist lone mothers to return to work or increase their hours, the first £15.00 of maintenance is disregarded, and thereafter family credit is reduced by 70p for every £1.00 of maintenance. This may indeed have helped some divorced or separated mothers in making the move from income support to family credit and earnings. Unfortunately, the very low incidence of maintenance payments to single mothers nationally, with just 14 per cent in receipt in 1991, and the low average weekly payment of £14.94, means that few single mothers benefit from this move.

The introduction of the Child Support Agency in 1993 was meant to ensure the payment of maintenance by errant fathers. Much was made of the potential penalties faced by young single mothers who might, for very good reasons, not wish to or be able to give information about the fathers of their children. However, regardless of whether the Child Support Agency intervenes, the real issues lie in the fact that the majority of the young men who fathered the children in this study could not have paid maintenance even if they wanted to, as they were unemployed. In this respect, the mothers felt that, although in principle young men did have a responsibility to provide for their children, any efforts to enforce this responsibility were unrealistic:

"Oh aye it's a good thing I suppose, well why shouldn't they have to pay out for them. It's not just the mother's responsibility. And it makes you feel bad knowing that you have to live on social all the time. I've told them where he [the father] lives and that but I can't see them getting owt out of him, 'cause he's never worked, well not properly. Anyway, he can't pay out for all of them can he [laughs]."

This mother was aware that the father of her child had fathered at least two other children to different women.

Why don't they work?

Although the majority say they would like to, many cannot work. Reasons for not working are many and varied, the most obvious being the lack of affordable child care and low wages, which in combination make many young single mothers worse off working than if they rely solely on benefits.

Child care

Single mothers have on average a higher proportion of children under school age than do divorced or separated mothers; thus they have a greater need for child care if they are to work even part time. In the Newcastle region private nursery places cost from £60.00 to £90.00 per week. Child minders are slightly less expensive, at around £10.00 per day, but still not within the reach of most young mothers. Although there are several social services nurseries in the area, they cater for families with a need for support, rather than simply providing day care to enable parents to work.

In October 1994, in an effort to assist families to make the transition from income support to family credit and earnings, or to increase their working hours, the government introduced help with child-care costs in the form of an earnings disregard in the calculation of family credit. The disregard offers a maximum income increase of £40 per family for those claiming a combination of family credit, housing benefit, disability working allowance and council tax benefit. For a mother claiming family credit alone it offers a maximum of £28 per week. Whilst this sum provides some help, it will hardly cover the true cost of full-time child care for even one child.

The majority of working mothers, both lone and otherwise, do not pay for child care at all but rely on informal care from partners, family and friends.[8] Of the sample mothers who were not working at the point of interview, only two reported having a family member who could look after their child if they worked. This is understandable if we take into account the fact that few of the mothers had any contact with the child's father, and thus no contact with paternal grandparents. They were therefore limited to their own family. Given the young age of the mothers, it is also likely that their own parents are still quite young, and may be working themselves, with no time to baby-sit. Additionally, as many mothers reported, there may still be younger siblings at home, and a mother may not feel she can ask her own mother to take on additional caring responsibilities.

Often mothers believe that they will be able to work once their child begins school full time. However, child-care problems do not become any less when a child is at school, simply different. Then a mother must find work to fit round school times, or someone to collect the child after school, which again she may have to pay for. She must cater also for school holidays and periods of illness. In a group discussion, one mother calculated that, although she was better off working than being on income support, on a weekly basis during term time all the financial benefit was negated by paying for holiday child care. Over a full year, she was actually worse off working. Although there are any number of 'open' playschemes to entertain children during school holidays, 'closed' full-day care schemes are very limited and costly. One lone parent organisation, Gingerbread, which had offered such care at no cost to the parent for over 12 years, has recently had to cease virtually all playschemes due to lack of funding. The small amount that lone parents in general can afford to pay would go no way towards the cost of the scheme, and alternative funding has become harder to find over recent years.

Term-time working

Mothers are acutely aware of the dangers their children face if left alone, and few leave them willingly. Some even give up jobs during the school holidays in order to care for their children:

"I couldn't leave mine, not where we live. They're OK, sensible like but the kids around and the grown ups too ... I just wouldn't trust anyone. If we lived somewhere else, a better part like, then I might leave them with a neighbour but not where we live, too much crime ... drugs and that."
(Lone mother in group discussion)

This mother worked during the school term and gave up her job every summer in order to look after her children. Unfortunately, this admirable attitude of trying to be self-sufficient, while also trying to be a good mother, is rewarded with further financial difficulties as she waits for the reinstatement of income support and full housing benefit each time she becomes unemployed.

Despite the Secretary of State's target times for local benefit agencies (DSS) to process income support claims (currently 71 per cent of claims to be dealt with in 5 days), in the Newcastle region these targets are seldom met and mothers can wait as long as several weeks. Working will also alter entitlement to housing benefit and, as has been discussed earlier, reinstatement of housing benefit can take several weeks, even months, as reported by welfare rights workers in some areas.

Low wages and the benefit trap

Despite high unemployment in the region, most of the sample mothers felt that they would be able to find some work, perhaps in a shop or bar, if they had child care. However, even when work can be found, it seldom brings in enough money to make working, especially part-time working, worthwhile, and many mothers said they felt they would not be able to earn enough to cover lost benefits:

"We could only do cleaning ... and that don't pay enough, not by the time you pay for baby sitters and that, wouldn't be worth it."

Compared to married mothers, lone mothers are significantly more likely to be employed in services such as cleaning and catering, and younger mothers more likely still, with the resulting greater likelihood of lower wages.[9]

Part-time working

A mother on income support can earn £15.00 per week before her earnings are deducted pound for pound from her benefit. Two of the three sample mothers who were working at the time of interview took advantage of this fact to boost their incomes, and worked less than 16 hours per week for no more than £15.00. If a mother works over 16 hours per week, she may claim family credit. However, as Louie Burghes pointed out in her study of lone parents in 1993, mothers can encounter a virtual earnings plateau.[10] As gross earnings increase a mother becomes liable for tax and national insurance contributions, while entitlement to housing benefit and family credit is reduced.

One of the women who worked less than 16 hours was employed to empty slot machines in a local amusement arcade. She worked 15 hours per week for £15. Not only does this display a tremendous willingness to work for very little pay in order to survive, but the fact that she saved virtually all this money in an attempt to put a little

aside for the future shows considerable discipline and determination to improve her lot in life.

The food budget

Of the sample mothers with only one child, the average amount spent on food and housekeeping each week was £19.00. Studies of families on low incomes show clearly a link between household poverty and a child's physical development. In 1989, the Department of Social Security found that boys receiving free school meals were, on average, shorter than other boys and that the height of school children was related to their diet.[11] A number of more recent research reports have highlighted the difficulties that lone parents who are financially dependent on income support have in meeting the nutritional needs of their dependent children.[12]

Asked what types of food they bought in a typical week, common answers were: tins of soup, beef burgers, tins of beans, fish fingers, chips and bread. Very few of the mothers bought fresh fruit or vegetables, even chips tended to be frozen, and few substituted meat with other forms of protein such as soya and pulses. Furthermore, the quality of the foods was in general lower than that which could have been purchased with a larger budget.

The food and alcohol budget prepared by King's College London for Bradshaw's 'Household Budgets and Living Standards' clearly set out a food budget and diet which would be conducive to long-term health and well being. It was clear from both group discussions and interviews that the mothers in the study fell far short of achieving this level of nutrition. Asked what she ate herself, one mother replied:

"Just a sandwich really, I don't get hungry, not really just make do with a bit of bread and that, some soup. Or if I go to my mate's and she might say have a sandwich here ... just that really."

Facilities

There is a popularly held belief that those on low incomes could feed themselves more adequately if they shopped and cooked more wisely, buying fresh foods rather than processed. However, this belief presupposes an easily available supply of fresh foods, a knowledge of what to do with them and a store cupboard full of standard ingredients and seasonings in order to make appetising meals. Young mothers in many cases have none of these.

Many mothers are restricted to the use of small local shops, mini markets and mobile food vans serving housing estates. Such retailers are expensive in comparison to larger supermarkets and town markets, and provide little in the way of fresh food, needing to stock less perishable items, often of the lowest quality. The supermarkets most favoured by the sample mothers were Kwik-Save and Netto. Even the mothers who used Netto regularly were aware of the low quality of the food it sold but felt that they were limited by the amount of money they could spend. Another attraction of cheaper food stores such as Netto is their location on or near estates and in poorer areas, thus eliminating the need for costly transport.

Whilst Newcastle has a good market, where fresh foods can be bought at reasonable prices, bus fares in order to reach it are often costly. A bus journey from one large Newcastle estate, Scotswood, where a high proportion of young mothers are housed, to the centre of the city where the markets and cut-price shops are to be found, costs over 80 pence each way, money which mothers feel would be better spent on immediate food. Few mothers have sufficient money to buy the less essential items of seasonings and standard ingredients such as rice, pasta or flour, and must concentrate their efforts on providing a meal for today rather than ingredients for tomorrow. Finally, mothers interviewed displayed very limited cooking skills. Cooking or domestic science has lost importance in the school curriculum over the years, and some mothers had few, if any, domestic and culinary skills passed to them from their own parents.

Help from friends and family

Many mothers, especially those who spent the least on food for their families, reported eating regularly at someone else's house, or having some form of help from family members with their food shopping. Perhaps a sister or parent provided two or three good meals each week:

"Aye, I go visit my Mam or our Shona [sister], just pop in like just for a natter, but it's always at meal times [laughs]. The bairns eat more at our Shona's than at home sometimes."

The mothers to whom this applied agreed that, if it were not for this regular assistance, their food bill would be considerably higher, causing greater budgeting problems. This type of assistance is perhaps masking the real level of poverty and struggle experienced by the young women.

Concern about nutrition

Health Visitors in the region are understandably concerned about the level of nutrition mothers and children are receiving. A report by Alison Cullen,[13] Newcastle's Chief Community Dietitian, outlines the severity of the problem in the area. The report studied the dietary behaviour and attitudes of young mothers and young pregnant women between the ages of 15 and 24 in the Newcastle region, bringing to light their lack of nutritional awareness and the difficulty with which they feed themselves and their children.

Health workers and others, including hostel workers, make concerted efforts to work with young mothers on health and nutrition-related subjects. However, group work of this kind is notoriously difficult to manage, with any number of factors from a rainy day, to lack of bus fare, to a fractious child and low self-esteem, preventing a mother from attending groups. One community midwife in the area who tried to set up a group for mothers to meet and support each other, while discussing nutrition and cooking, did not receive one visitor to the sessions in eight weeks, despite heavy advertising in an area of high single parent population. Schemes such as 'Community Mothers' in the USA and similar projects in England such as 'Home Start', which aim to offer one-to-one support and training for young mothers, are more successful but require committed funding and management.

Making ends meet

In his study of household budgets and living standards in 1993, Jonathan Bradshaw found income support fell £25.00 a week short of the amount needed for a lone parent with two children to achieve even a low cost budget.[14] This shortfall was felt strongly by the single mothers in the study, many expressing real difficulties in making ends meet, even under normal circumstances. In some cases this difficulty literally resulted in not having enough to eat:

"... the bairn always gets plenty ... I see to that like ... but I don't think I do. Well I know I don't not really. That's why I'm tired all the time and ratty, get dead ratty these days ... can't be bothered with nowt."

Asked how much extra they needed each week to make living on income support easier, the most common answer was £10.00. Some women felt that it was not so much the amount of income support that caused the real problem, as its rigid nature. Many women reported frequently having to borrow just £5 from a friend or relative to see them over a difficult few days. They would have preferred to be able to access some of the following weeks benefit:

"... don't need a lot really, I don't think. You can manage on a normal week right up to the last day, well I can. But I never have nowt left on Wednesday [last day before benefit on Thursday], not usually. I always have to borrow a couple of quid off my Mam or my Gran. But it's when something goes wrong and you have to pay out extra, like for shoes for the bairn. I tried putting something away but I'd spent it before the end of the week, can't save nothing."

"If you could just get a little extra some weeks, like when it's double on a holiday, that's a help. I go and do a right big shop, if I don't need to pay owt off."

In general, women budgeted well with their money, the younger ones having the most difficulty. Most, however, said that by the last day or two prior to benefit day they had no more than one or two pounds left in their purses. Some had no money at all for the last two days. Only three of the sample mothers reported ever having money left at the end of the week to carry over to the new week or put away as savings. Seven said they always owed money to a friend or relative by the time they collected their benefit.

For those who were not having fuel cost taken directly from their income support, borrowing or 'robbing Peter to pay Paul' was common. When in difficulties, mothers will often miss a week's payment for gas or electricity. This did not cause a problem in most cases, and the missed payment was usually made up the following week. Problems arise, however, when, for one reason or another, two or three weeks payments are missed in order to cater for an emergency or unforeseen expense. Of the sample mothers 18 said they were, or had been, in difficulties at some time with their fuel payments.

Whereas fuel arrears would at one time have resulted in disconnection, the number of disconnections nationally has fallen dramatically in recent years, from 98,894 in 1979/80 to 23,693 in 1991/2. This is due largely to the introduction of key and token meters and the increase in the number of fuel direct payments from income support. However, these methods of fuel debt recovery may disguise the difficulties faced by those on low incomes. Fourteen of the 31 mothers

in the study were already paying for fuel directly out of their income support at source (22 said they would prefer fuel bills and water rates paid this way). As this arrangement cannot be made until fuel arrears have been incurred, the resulting payments are higher than they would be simply for the current fuel consumption as they include the arrears. In 1992/3, a total of 6,231 income support claimants in Newcastle had deductions from benefits for fuel arrears at an average payment of £9.86 for electricity and £9.31 for gas per week. It is not known what percentage were single mothers.

Five of the mothers used key meters in order to pay for their fuel and account for their arrears. (Again, with this method, the meter is set at a tariff high enough to account for the arrears; thus, current consumption of fuel becomes more expensive.) Mothers who have difficulties in paying this higher charge may effectively disconnect themselves, by not buying or using sufficient fuel for their real needs, only heating the home when the children are in and cutting back on hot water or cooking costs. It has long been noted by community centre workers that the busiest times are cold days in winter, when lone parents and others on low incomes can benefit from someone else's heating. None of the mothers in the study had ever been disconnected from a fuel supply, though several felt their fuel debts to be difficult, even unmanageable in some cases:

"... only mean to miss the odd one ... just if you can't manage one week but catching up's the problem. I had to borrow off my Nan just to catch up. Now I owe her, and she can't afford neither ... nobody's got no money in my family like ... they'd help if they could."

Weekly payment of water rates also offers the mothers an opportunity to cope with fluctuations in living costs. Twenty-seven of the study mothers said they missed the occasional payment for water. Water seems less likely to be disconnected, in the mothers' eyes, than gas or electricity. However, it can be the cause of rent arrears in some cases. Although housing benefit is paid directly to the landlord, the mother is responsible for her own water rates. Failure to pay can result in a suspended possession order. If such an order is broken, and payments are not made, it can lead to eviction. It is more likely to lead to an order for direct payment from benefit, and there was a total of 304 such orders in 1992/3 in Newcastle.

Credit and debt

When unforeseen expenses crop up and no amount of juggling of income support can help, mothers often use credit, which can in turn lead to debt. Berthoud and Kempson, in 1992, identified three debt-inducing factors: age, children, and income.[15] The risk of debt was higher if any two of these factors occurred. They noted that lone parents were particularly at risk of debt, with three times the number of problem debts as childless single people. The need for credit is by no means restricted to those on low incomes, but access to low cost credit is restricted to those on higher incomes and with a higher level of credit-worthiness. The assessment of credit-worthiness is based on employment, income, occupation and tenure. Thus, a young single mother with no employment, restricted to income support, and without assets such as property, has little access to the cheaper sources of bank or building society credit or credit cards. She is restricted to the more expensive check trading, such as Provident, to mail order or to money lenders both licensed and unlicensed.

The social fund

Social fund loans, the Government's own form of credit to those on low incomes, has come under criticism, not least for the added financial burden it puts on those already living in poverty. Indebtedness to the social fund has been growing since its introduction, but it remains a major source of financial help to lone parents on income support. The repayment of loans often puts even greater strain on a mother's budget. The average social fund loan repayment in 1991 was £5.53 per week, and few mothers can deduct this amount from income support without getting into further difficulty. In Newcastle during 1992/3 there were 16,992 applications to the social fund; the percentage of which were from young single mothers is unknown. Only 8,431 of these, less than 50 per cent, were successful. A mother who is unsuccessful may be forced to turn to other forms of credit:

"They [Social Fund Officers] knocked me back for a loan for a new washer. My old one packed in and they said it couldn't be mended, not right, it would go again like ... Well, so, now I go to the launderette every week with the big stuff, or to my sisters, if someone will take me. Thing is, it costs nearly a fiver at the wash, well I could have paid off the loan by now with that couldn't I? Going to get one from her club book [another mother in group] when I've paid off what I owe, couple of weeks, that'll be real then!"

Other forms of credit

Licensed money lenders, Check Traders (Provident) and Credit Drapers selling goods door-to-door on credit are sources of finance some of the young mothers resort to in many cases. In a study of families living on benefit on Tyneside, Bradshaw and Holmes noted that over half had existing credit arrangements with Check Traders, averaging £196.[16] Others had borrowed from money lenders. Of the mothers in this study, nine had taken a loan with a licensed money lender, or had had dealings with Provident, at some point. The problem arises not with the amount of the original loan or credit arrangement but with the length of time it takes to repay it at an affordable weekly amount. With typical APR ranging from 60 to 200 per cent for a Check Trader and up to 500 per cent for a licensed loan, a small amount of credit becomes a long and expensive debt.[17]

It is not uncommon for a mother to resort to a loan in order to consolidate several smaller problem debts, such as catalogue payments, debts to friends or family and arrears of fuel or water. The loan clears the debts; however, the debts were originally due to insufficient income, rather than bad management on the part of the mother. Now, with new loan repayments, income is reduced still further and the original debts soon return. When loan repayments become problematic, most reputable loan companies will negotiate, and in such cases some form of advocacy, such as a welfare rights organisation, is helpful. Welfare rights workers in the area report licensed loan companies being reasonable when a client falls behind with payments, and arrangements for reduced weekly payments are usually the answer. Unfortunately, not all loans are from licensed lenders.

Catalogue shopping is very common amongst young single mothers as a way of providing decent quality clothing and baby equipment for their children, as well as presents at Christmas. Whilst they are happy to wear cast-offs themselves, most mothers take great pride in providing for their children, and would rather go into debt than dress their child in second-hand clothes. Resulting debts of up to several hundred pounds on each of two or three catalogues were reported by Money Matters debt counselling agency in Newcastle. Over 50 per cent of the sample mothers had either run a catalogue themselves or bought items from a friend's catalogue at some point.

Catalogues are used also as a means of generating cash in an emergency. Items can be bought from the catalogue and sold for cash long before the purchase has been paid for. Most of the interview mothers knew of someone who did this regularly.

Loan sharks

The incidence of unlicensed money lending and loan sharking is difficult to estimate, surrounded as it is in secrecy and to an extent fear. Whilst loan sharks obviously do operate in many areas of any large city, few will admit to using them. In interviews, mothers occasionally referred to 'lenders' and 'Tally Men' from whom they occasionally borrowed:

"If I get short I'll have to borrow like ... just a tenner one week and pay back twenty next."

"Twenty! That's a lot! I only have to give them £15 for a tenner. Mind, I don't know what it'd be if I couldn't pay it back like ... I'd not pay twenty back, I'd sooner starve ... That's too much ... well I think."

This first mother was referring to a local money lender on her estate to whom she could turn if she ran out of money. Others in the group knew this to be common and felt that, although 100 per cent per week was not unusual, it was too high; 50 per cent seemed reasonable to them. In this case the mother did not need to set down anything as security; presumably the fact that she was known to the family was sufficient. However, not all 'lenders' are as trusting. In group interviews, cases were discussed openly of mothers who had handed their benefit books to loan sharks, who met them outside the post office each benefit day to ensure prompt and certain payment. It would appear from other studies that this is a common situation.[18]

10 Support

Infrastructures

The general public perception of the lives of young single mothers would seem to be contradictory. Either they live lonely, isolated lives in tower blocks, with few friends and no family support, or they congregate in groups in town centres and shopping malls, spending the day socialising with others. Both pictures are true to a certain extent, in that many mothers do lead very isolated lives and others do find support in the company of their peers. However, for the majority, life is a jigsaw of odd pieces of support and assistance from many sources, with spells of isolation and emotional turmoil.

The disjointed nature of this support is problematic and should be a cause for concern, especially in more rural areas, where it is most limited. Recent years have seen a growth in community development and social support for those living in inner cities. In the Newcastle region and in North Tyneside, City Challenge money has benefited many in more deprived areas. However, the isolation and need for support felt by different groups in rural environments is often overlooked, possibly in the belief that small towns and rural areas still have a 'community spirit', or because the numbers of those in need may be smaller. In the words of one 17 year old mother from Castle Morpeth:

"There's not a lot of young mums round here, not as young as me anyway, and they mostly have blokes. People look at you funny. I can't go anywhere to meet other mums 'cause there isn't any where. It's just me and the baby all day, some times I go to my Mum's, if she's not working but I've got no friends."

Where it exists at all, the professional support of young single mothers is all too often offered on a 'here it is, come and get it' basis. However, there is a whole range of factors which limit a young woman's ability to access and make use of professional support. They include physical distance, lack of money, practical child-care problems, lack of confidence and low self-esteem.

These problems are exacerbated by the lack of specialist understanding on the problems and attitudes of young single mothers, their boyfriends and families.

In the early days of pregnancy and new motherhood, support is provided generally by health visitors and midwifes. This may be nothing more than ante-natal classes or baby-weighing clinics but it is a point of contact with other mothers and advisers. It is here that vital work is done around basic parenting and baby care. Breast feeding, now recognised as so beneficial to both mother and child, is promoted by health visitors to all mothers. The response amongst young single mothers is poor, and a growing cause for concern. This negative attitude to breast feeding is highlighted in other studies on young motherhood.[19]

In later months or years, there are some mother and toddler groups, or pre-school play groups in city areas, although less so in more rural districts. Unfortunately, many of the younger mothers, often most in need of support, feel excluded from these groups because of their age, as has been noted by other research:[20]

"I don't [go to a local support group]. They look at you like you're a slag. ... cause I was so young like ... 15 when I had her. It's for older mothers, they're all older you know, 20 and that."

"They only want you to go so they can tell you how to be a good mother ... tell you what to do and that."

Whilst this young woman was a mother, she was still a young teenager who felt that the local group did not cater for her needs. This attitude was common amongst the sample mothers, with only five attending any support or social group regularly, although 14 did know of one. Others researching mothers in this young age group have found similar stories.[21]

The support most mothers require to become independent mothers falls into two categories. Initially they require practical assistance, such as transport and physical help with gardening, decorating and moving furniture in. This immediate identifiable need often overshadows the greater need for companionship, reassurance and help with parenting, budgeting and emotional difficulties.

Although health and social workers are to be commended for their efforts to provide support, it must be recognised that, to a great extent, they are doing so as a small part of their overall duties, usually without specific training in the problems and attitudes of young single mothers and without funds for the job. The health and social workers who took part in this study felt that, despite their efforts, they could not provide a suitable level of support. Given the 24-hour-a-day nature of parenting, many mothers, especially the youngest ones and those without family support, need 24-hour assistance, if only by telephone. Mothers frequently commented that the evenings and nights were their most stressful times both in terms of mothering and for their own emotional stability. It is at this time when mothers lose the support of their peers, who, without money, transport and baby-sitters, are also confined to their own homes with their own small children.

One 16 year old mother, worried about the health of her little boy, took the child one night in a taxi to the local casualty department. The illness turned out to be minor and she was chastised by the hospital workers for wasting time:

"They just think you know what to do ... I don't know, the bairn's only little and I got a right scare, there was no one to ask."

Naturally the need for support is greatest in the early months, when young mothers are, like any new parent, unsure of how to look after their new babies, and both mother and child are recovering from birth. However, a developing child passes through many difficult stages, of which many young mothers have no understanding. It is fair to say that many young mothers have unrealistic perceptions of what mothering entails and of the needs of a small child.

The need for guidance and support is not limited to mothers with babies. Indeed, many mothers find the first few months easier than subsequent months or years, when a child becomes more demanding. Mothers in the study often reported having 'hyper active' children. The consensus of opinion amongst health visitors, however, is that a good deal of this 'hyper activity' is nothing more than normal childhood energy, coupled with boredom. Unfortunately, the existing

support networks, already over-stretched, tend not to be able to grow with their client's changing needs and assist young mothers to develop their mothering skills as a child grows. Many of the study mothers with older children said they no longer saw their health visitor once they stopped taking the child to be weighed. In many cases, the health visitor had been the only professional support they had.

Within a relationship, the stress of new parenthood can be shared with a partner. There is a greater likelihood also of there being a second set of grandparents to offer assistance and respite when needed. For many young mothers the worries and problems can be shared with no one other than her own parents, and for some even this support is denied. Those working with young women are increasingly concerned about the growing number of young women with no family support at all, who remain almost invisible due to their extreme isolation.

A support initiative being tried in some areas of the country, and more commonly in the United States, is that of 'Community Mothering'. This system draws on the skills and experience of existing mothers in the community and encourages them, with training and some payment, to take over the role of supporter to younger mothers.

Community Mothers are expected to make regular visits on the young mothers assigned to them and are paid per visit. The use of members of the community in this way overcomes some of the barriers which prevent young women from approaching professionals for support. It also eliminates the need for a geographical 'centre' such as a clinic, which can in itself become a barrier.

Community Mothers are responsible for encouraging young mothers to take up child health checks and vaccinations and for introducing them to other support networks, generally assisting and encouraging the younger women.

Young mothers who are eventually housed some distance from their families may well not have the benefit of a telephone, and easy access to someone within the community is of great help in times of stress or difficulty.

Recent survey data show that less than 54 per cent of all lone parent families with one child have a telephone. In Newcastle, a City Challenge monitoring report (1992) found a telephone connection rate of only 26 per cent on the Cruddas Park council estate, an estate with a significantly high proportion of lone parents:

"It's worse at night, I don't like it at night … If something happens you know. There's only the neighbours, I suppose I could knock them up but you don't like do you. No one in our family's got a phone or a car."

One reason for so few single mothers having a telephone is the high installation cost – as discussed in the previous chapter, this is another instance of a one-off payment which cannot be accommodated within a tight weekly budget.

The benefits of a telephone for social support and access to emergency services are obvious, as families become more scattered and lone parent families increase. However, the wider implications of being denied this most basic form of communication are often overlooked. Many of the welfare services used by young mothers are increasingly available only by phone. Without access to a telephone, many mothers expend considerable energy, time and money making fruitless trips to the housing department, welfare office or voluntary advice group, when a simple phone call would suffice. The need is greater still in rural areas, where support services are more thinly spread and bus services are poorer. In Northumberland, and some areas of Castle Morpeth and Blyth Valley, the voluntary sector has made few inroads and what services exist are targeted at the larger towns. Here, in the absence of well-developed outreach support, the need for a telephone is paramount.

Mothers who make the transition to independence from a mother and baby hostel, or local authority care, are at greatest risk of isolation and in greatest need of support. In many cases these mothers have no one else to turn to except hostel workers because their relationship with their family has broken down. Many find leaving the hostel difficult. Hostel workers frequently become involved with the mothers outside of work hours and are called on at all time of the night and day. Hostel workers consider aftercare and outreach work to be of highest priority, but few are funded for this vital part of their work. There is a growing awareness amongst accommodation providers in the region that without the development of outreach support schemes, the provision of housing alone may create as many problems as it cures. In 'Residential Care of Young Single Mothers', Trish Skuse highlights the importance of thorough resettlement work and notes how difficult such support schemes are to fund.[22]

Relationships

Very few of the mothers in the study had maintained a relationship of any sort with the father of their child. Indeed, few could see any reason to do so for the child's sake, or their own, passing comments on the fathers' unemployment, lack of stability or in some cases their violent nature:

"… can't do nothing … bloody useless, can't leave the bairn with him or nothing. He never gives me any money when he's here. Just hangs around a while, then gets nasty, starts hitting me and leaves. I'll not have him back this time."

However, it must be remembered that the mothers are still young women, many are teenagers, with a natural interest in boyfriends. Many also suffer extremely low self-esteem, which is raised considerably when a boy takes an interest in them. A boyfriend offers companionship, improved self-image and, in some cases, may be of limited practical or financial assistance. For these reasons and many more, most of the mothers did feel a boyfriend played an important role in their lives. However, many experienced very difficult and turbulent relationships, and frequent changes of partner were common.

This increase in the number of partners, especially in cohabiting relationships, is giving rise to great concern amongst health and social workers. Recent research is beginning to show the effects of family disruption and frequent partner changing on the development of young children.[23] Health visitors taking part in this study commented on the problems caused when young mothers changed their parenting practices due to emotional stress or to fit the requirements of a new boyfriend. A small child becomes extremely confused and difficult when, what was allowed yesterday, results in a smack today, because the mother wants to keep a new boyfriend happy. It must be stressed, however, that the vast majority of young mothers care for their children extremely well, and the mothers in the study displayed great love and affection towards their babies.

New relationships bring with them the risk of a subsequent pregnancy. A young woman involved in an ongoing relationship and aware that she is sexually active may well take precautions to prevent pregnancy. However, a woman who is not expecting to have sex, as she has no regular partner, is less likely to be so well-prepared. Furthermore, given the very low self-esteem of many of the mothers, some will not feel they wish to refuse a partner simply because neither has condoms instantly to hand. Anecdotal evidence from conversations with mothers suggested that many became pregnant the first time they had sexual intercourse with the child's father. This pattern could well repeat itself for subsequent pregnancies. As discussed by Hudson and Ineichen in *Taking it Lying Down*[24] there are other reasons for subsequent pregnancies, most relating in some way to the way young women view themselves in the world.

Not all young mothers of course experience such difficulties with boyfriends. Within the study, those young women with strong family connections, who visited or were visited by their parents frequently, tended to be happy to live alone with their child and to spend the next few years building a home and life together. This re-enforces the concern about the difficulties faced by young mothers coming out of care. During the study, those mothers who were not independent but who were living in mother and baby hostels awaiting assessment by social services, were revisited on a number of occasions. In all three cases, they had very limited family support, and, despite the immense efforts of the hostel workers to prepare them for independent life with their babies, only one ever made the move to independence with her child. The others had their children taken for fostering for various reasons. The one mother who made the move found the transition extremely difficult and, even after she had been given a house, took several months to actually leave the hostel. This difficulty is common, and demonstrates the need to develop satisfactory after-care services for mothers leaving both care and hostel situations, to replace the support which would normally come from a family.

Relationships – the broader view

There is a belief, held by many, that some young women are having a succession of babies fathered by different men. This study uncovered the reverse, that there are young men who father a succession of children to different women, and show no responsibility to any of them. The following comment arose during one of the group discussions:

"... others, oh aye. Well there was this girl I went to school with. She had a bairn [by him] a couple of month before [me]. I heard he's got another lass caught on too."

As with other studies of single parents, this research has focused on the mothers. However, no discussion on single motherhood can take place without asking the question 'where are the fathers?'. Of the women interviewed for this research, only two out of the 31 had retained any 'real' contact with the fathers of their children. The relationships were brought to an end sometimes by the mothers themselves, often due to violence. However, more often it was the men who simply faded into the distance without taking any responsibility, financial or otherwise, for their children. This raises two important issues:

(i) What has happened in the lives of young men that they feel so little responsibility towards their children?

(ii) Why, given the highly publicised aims of the Child Support Agency, are so few young men paying any maintenance?

The answers to both these question must lie in the economy and employment. Responsibility brings with it demands which must be met. Without employment, young men have no resources with which to meet these demands. Noticeably, the only father in the study who had retained a relationship with his child and its mother was the only one in regular employment. He was also the only one from whom the Child Support Agency were collecting maintenance.

Young mothers for their part can see no point in putting up with what was a less than satisfactory relationship, if they were not going to be supported by the man emotionally, nor financially if he is unemployed.

Whilst many mothers recognised that there might be a role for a 'father figure' in their child's life, that figure was not to be found in the young men they were familiar with. Sadly many were written off as 'bloody useless ... can't do nothing'.

It should not be assumed that young women have given up on the idea of long-term, responsible relationships or even marriage. They are simply realistic in seeing that many young men have nothing to offer in the way of finance, domestic or caring skills.

Perhaps much of the cause of teenage motherhood can be linked to the low confidence and self-esteem of young women and their lack of employment prospects. If so, much of the cause of the women having to take over full responsibility for the resulting child must similarly be linked to poor employment prospects of young men. Until such time as economic, employment and education opportunities give young men the ability to earn a living and be responsible for themselves, issues around maintenance and responsibility for their children are irrelevant.

11 Conclusions to Part II

Whilst few of the sample mothers, seven in all, had given up their first tenancies to return to the family home or to other accommodation, many considered doing so for a range of reasons. Ultimately, regardless of her age, the determining factor in how easily a mother became settled into independent living was the amount of support she received. A very young mother, able to access a strong family network for daily support, can settle in her independent home quite quickly, whereas an older mother without such a network may find it harder. The following sections offer some summary comments on the problems young single mothers encounter in maintaining their first home.

Housing

Dissatisfaction with housing stems almost entirely from the social problems of the area, and the distance from the mothers family, rather than the actual property.

There is a conflict between the housing and area a single mother and her family will ultimately need, in comparison to the type of housing she is able to manage and maintain in the first months or years of independence.

The lack of accommodation for young men is enticing some into casual cohabiting relationships with young mothers who have their own tenancies.

Finance

Income support is too low, even at its highest rate, to meet anything other than the normal weekly living costs. It does not allow for larger one-off expenses, such as purchase of a bed for a growing child or even to cover emergency replacement of faulty home equipment.

When the social fund does assist with one-off expenses, it is in the form of a loan, the repayment of which puts considerable strain on an already insufficient income. The high weekly repayment rate is making mothers less inclined to apply for social fund loans, and more likely to opt for other forms of credit, such as catalogue shopping, which is more expensive in the long run but cheaper on a weekly basis.

The Child Support Agency is failing to ensure payment of maintenance to this group of mothers despite the mother's willingness to give information.

Whilst employment in difficult for all lone parents, a range of factors makes this sub group of lone parents less likely to be able to improve their situation through work than any other; they include:

- limited work experience;

- low incidence of maintenance;

- greater need for child care;

- less likelihood of child care from family.

The majority of mothers managed their finances extremely well under the circumstances. They did so, however, by going without themselves in order to provide for their children. It is likely that the real level of poverty experienced by the young women is masked by their determination to provide well for their children.

Support

From the community

First, it should be remembered that many of this group of mothers are still teenage girls. Their personal needs, quite apart form their needs as mothers, are very different to those of women five years older, in their early twenties. Most felt that what community support there was for mothers, was not for them. If they are to be reached with certain messages about parenting and nutrition, for instance, the messages must be presented in a language they understand; currently they are not. It is plain that the accepted policy, of providing support in group work situations, is not successful with this group of young mothers.

Statutory services

Social services are failing to provide any preventative support in Newcastle. Youth agencies are concentrating on young single people, especially men. Health visitors, whilst they are the most used support providers, are limited in the support they can give, and their services tend to be used only while the child is a baby. Unless a mother has subsequent pregnancies, contact with health visitors will be lost after the child reaches school age, if not before.

There is insufficient after-care provided for mothers leaving care or temporary mother and baby hostels, resulting in these women finding it more difficult to adjust to independence. It is this group who would most benefit from the development of 'second stage' accommodation, providing independence with accessible support day and night.

Notes to Part II

1 Department of the Environment (1991). *English House Conditions Survey 1991*. HMSO (London)

2 Joseph Rowntree Foundation (1994). *Mulit-agency working on difficult-to-manage estates*. Joseph Rowntree Foundation (York)

3 Payne, J. and Payne, G. (1977). 'Housing Pathways and Stratification: a study of life chances in the housing market', *Journal of Social Policy* No.6

4 Cohen, R., Coxall, J. and Sadiq-Sangster, A. (1992). *Hardship Britain, Being Poor in the 1990s*. CPAG (London)

5 Burghes, L. and Brown, M. (1995, forthcoming). *Single Mothers: problems, prospects and policies*. Family Policy Study Centre (London); also for further examples: Hudson, F. and Ineichen, B. (1992). *Taking it Lying Down – Sexuality and Teenaged Motherhood*. Macmillan (London)

6 Haskey, J. (1991). 'Estimated Number and Demographic Characteristics of One Parent Families In Great Britain', *Population Trend No. 65*. OPCS (London)

7 Bradshaw, J. and Millar, J. (1991). *Lone Parent Families in the UK*. HMSO (London)

8 Office of Population Censuses and Surveys (1994). *Daycare Services for Children*. OPCS (London)

9 *Population Trends No.72*. OPCS (London)

10 Burghes, L. (1993). *One Parent Families – Policy Options for the 1990s*. Family Policy Study Centre (London)

11 See for example Oppenheim, C. (1993). *Poverty: The Facts* CPAG (London); Cole-Hamilton, I. *Poverty Can Seriously Damage Your Health*

12 B. Dobson *et al.* (1995) *Diet, Choice and Poverty* and Dowler, E. and Calvert, C. (1995). *Nutrition and Diet in Lone Parent Families in London*, both published by the Family Policy Studies Centre (London)

13 Cullen, A. *Nutrition in Pregnancy and Early Family Life: Attitudes, Beliefs and Behaviour.* An unpublished study by Newcastle's Chief Community Dietitian

14 Bradshaw, J. (1993). *Household Budgets and Living Standards*. Joseph Rowntree Foundation (York)

15 Berthoud, R. and Kempson, E. (1992). *Credit and Debt in Britain, The PSI Report*. Policy Studies Institue (London)

16 Bradshaw, J. and Holmes, H. (1989) *Living on the Edge - A study of living standard of families living on benefit in Tyne and Wear*. Child Poverty Action Group (London)

17 Ford, J. (1991) *Consuming Credit, Debt and Poverty in the UK*. Child Poverty Action Group (London)

18 *Ibid*

19 Skuse, T. (forthcoming) Trust for the Study of Adolescence (Brighton)

20 *Ibid*; also see Hudson, F. and Ineichen, B. (1992) (note 5)

21 Skuse (forthcoming) (Note 17)

22 *Ibid*

23 See for example Burghes, L. (1994). *Lone Parents and Family Disruption – The Outcomes for Children*. Occasional Paper, Family Policy Study Centre (London)

24 Hudson and Ineichen (1992) (note 5)

Part III
Policy options

Policy options

The housing and support needs of a large proportion of young single mothers in the Newcastle region are not being met. The difficulty these young women face in setting up and maintaining an independent home is exacerbated by the fact that existing policies do not recognise the different needs and abilities of this sub-group of lone parents.

Accepting that options are constrained both by financial considerations and by a long-standing moral determination not to condone or support activity likely to encourage young women to have children at the expense of the taxpayer, there are nevertheless several areas of existing policy which might offer solutions to some of their problems.

General

Of paramount importance to this group of young mothers is the level of support they receive in the early days of independence. For a small minority, some of those leaving mother and baby hostels, or coming out of care pregnant or with babies, this may mean heavily supported staged accommodation, easing them into independence. For others, the majority, the solutions to their problems lie in policies which will assist them to make the most of existing accommodation and finance, whilst at the same time meshing them into the community and existing support networks, such as community groups, credit unions, tenant groups and training schemes.

Policy makers are understandably fearful of being seen to treat young single mothers more favourably than other families. However, social policy may need to recognise that some of them may be more vulnerable than are other families, less experienced and with fewer resources. Perhaps it is time to reconsider Finer's 'special group'[1], and consider policies which will help young single mothers overcome their adversities and, more importantly, help their children thrive.

Housing

In an ideal world, local authorities would have sufficient housing stock for all who wanted it; as it is they cannot provide for all who need it, not even for all who need it urgently. Accepting that a great increase in the building of new 'general purpose' council properties is unlikely, what should be done to improve access to decent family housing for young single mothers?

We might start by looking at the recently proposed notion that young single mothers should have their access to local authority housing restricted still further, by being required to remain within the family home until such time as they have reached the top of the local authority waiting list, and that, in order for them to leave earlier, families might have to go to court. This idea is proposed by the DOE in its paper on Access to Local Authority and Housing Association Tenancies (1994).

Leaving aside the worst situations of family violence and abuse, this idea presupposes that the family home and income can actually accommodate the mother and her baby. It may not, moreover, be in the best interests of the family, either the original one, or the new one. This policy may fail to recognise the stress to which many families are already subjected, in terms of lack of space, financial problems and relationship difficulties. Nor does it take into account the possibility that the family home might be completely incompatible with the needs of a new baby. Finally, it does not recognise the length of time families might have to endure these unsatisfactory conditions. Circumstances that all members of the family may be able to live with for a few weeks, or a month or two, may be unendurable for the year or two that a mother may spend on the waiting list.

The housing trap

One of the major difficulties faced by anyone housed under homeless legislation is the 'one offer trap'. Given the current shortage of property and the difficulty of obtaining a transfer to an alternative property, the current policy, which forces homeless single mothers to accept the first property they are offered, also condemns them to remain in it for many years. Many mothers, although technically facing homelessness, can remain, for a short while at least, in their current accommodation if they must. In this light, giving mothers at least some choice of tenancies, might prevent them 'jumping out of the frying pan into the fire' by swapping one unsuitable accommodation for another equally unsuitable but more permanent one. The introduction of a housing welfare officer might allow for a more long-term overview of the needs of the family before a tenancy is offered.

'Housing careers'

We must recognise that the housing needs of a family headed by a young single mother are no more immutable than those of a two parent family; if anything they may be more changeable. A single mother family like other families should be able to develop a 'pathway' to improved housing, depending on its changing needs and aspirations. With allocation policy so heavily based on space requirements, it is difficult, however, for a young woman to improve her housing situation through transfers if she does not need more space.

It may be that this problem can never be fully resolved until such time as there is renewed investment in social housing. An interim policy which acknowledges people's needs to transfer for a range of reasons, even if they are 'suitably' housed according to policy, is needed to provide some respite. Encouraging and assisting mutual exchanges might help this to a degree, but it is unlikely to assist a young mother to move from a particularly 'difficult to let' area to a better one. One possibility might be to give greater recognition to 'emotional need' and 'emotional stress' within the points-based system for accommodation transfers.

Housing associations

Given, in general, the better quality of housing association property, young single mothers and their children would benefit from increased access to it. It is not entirely clear why young single mothers are so poorly represented in housing association property, although there was some evidence from the present study of their being excluded from it. Further reseach and policy initiatives should be considered. In the meantime, young mothers need to be made fully aware, by local authority housing officers, of the options available to them.

Private rented sector

Whilst the private rented sector is never likely to rival the public sector in the provision of housing, to enhance or improve their role, single mothers and their children might be encouraged by:

- Improved relations between housing benefit, social services departments and private landlords.

- Private renting being made more attractive to young mothers by improving the quality of property and the service by landlords.

- Consideration of a scheme to address the problems that low income families face in meeting deposits and 'rent in advance' required by the private rented sector.

A package of support

Getting accommodation, as the report shows, is not the end of the story for a young mother trying to establish an independent home for herself and her child. Maintaining that home and caring for a young child is another and equally difficult matter. Young mothers need advice and information on a range of other issues, notably social security, and arguably access to less tangible social support as well.

Some 'welfare' policy embracing these diverse elements would help prevent a situation in which young mothers are left to fend for themselves on large, often isolated housing estates which are frequently ill-provided with community facilities. Devising such a policy, however, would not necessarily be an easy matter.

As the local authority is the main port of call for young single mothers seeking secure housing, this contact between young mother and a statutory agency could be used to greater effect.

Currently, young women in many towns and cities simply pass through housing offices as nothing more than another applicant. Their needs for anything other than bricks, mortar, and a certain number of bedrooms are generally not recognised by – nor are they the business of – busy housing officers. A mother's voluntary contact with the housing department offers an ideal opportunity to introduce her to a fully trained welfare officer, who could take on the responsibility not only for her housing but for many aspects of her welfare.

This might develop from the training of existing housing managers, or it might be better provided by entirely different members of staff who could draw together the elements of housing, welfare rights and health into a package to suit the needs of a particular young woman. It may be the case that this support might be provided by voluntary agencies with specific skills and knowledge of young single parent's problems, following a refferal from the local authority.

On a somewhat smaller scale parenting and basic life skills as well as more general social support could be provided through a system of support (such as Community Mothering) by existing community organisations with the experience and expertise to develop them.

Finance

Income support

Numerous reports reiterate the inadequate level of income support for families. Not only does it fail to provide an adequate standard of living on a weekly basis, but entrenches young mothers in debt from which it is impossible to escape because of the same low weekly income. The cycle which follows, of low-income debt-repayment of debt-reduced income, often begins at the very earliest point in independence. It is at this point that young mothers face greatly increased living expenses in trying to equip a home and provide for a young baby.

In addition to the problems income support poses for all families with dependent children, living and running an established home are not as great as the weekly cost of living whilst establishing that home. Newly independent young mothers therefore have a particularly difficult financial problem.

A range of wholesale and piecemeal solutions have been proposed over the years. They include increasing benefit rates – whether income support or child or one parent benefit – or the introduction of a non-means-tested benefit for lone parents. Some raise difficulties of financial cost and equity of treatment with other families with children.

One method of providing for such expenses might be to make occasional supplementary payments in addition to benefit, as standard, throughout the year. Making perhaps two or four payments would enable a mother to plan ahead, or to deal with emergencies as they arise, rather than having to seek more costly credit. A recently published report suggests an annual or biennial lump sum of £50-£100.[2]

Maternity payment

The current £100 maternity payment does not meet the true cost of providing the basic essentials for a new baby. Whilst many mothers ignore their own needs, or the needs of their home, they cannot ignore the needs of their babies. They often have to go into debt, or use social fund money meant for their home, to provide the basics. Like all first-time low income mothers they and their babies would benefit from an increase in the payment.

Social fund

Young mothers find nothing good to say about the social fund. Rather they feel it fails to provide adequately for them as they try to establish a home for their children. To them, the fund seems neither consistent, nor fair; it may well not be cost effective in real terms either, given the financial strain on those repaying loans.[3]

For the mothers in this study the previous system of single payments had certain advantages. One obvious one is its implicit acknowledgement that, if people need financial assistance, it is because they are poor, and, if they are poor, they cannot afford to repay loans without becoming poorer. This is no less true of young single mothers establishing a home today.

The need for loans

As many mothers do run their lives effectively on informal credit from family and friends, or more formal and more costly, small-scale credit from licensed lenders, there is clearly a need for this low level of borrowing. Income support is not flexible enough to cater for the very minor fluctuations in weekly living costs, in the way that someone in employment might be assisted by an overdraft facility. If the structure of income support is not to be made more flexible then the greater development of Credit Unions would offer access to safer and cheaper credit for many mothers, whilst at the same time drawing them into the support networks of older women on estates and in community groups from whom they currently feel alienated.

What of the future?

It is both heartening and distressing to see that so many young single mothers have not given up hope of taking control, gaining employment and some measure of self-sufficiency and independence from social security. It is heartening because it refutes the idea that they belong to a group in society who have shelved all responsibility for their lives and needs and are prepared to scrounge off the state for ever more.

It is distressing because it is hard to see how they are ever going to realise their goals of employment, a better home and improved standard of living.

The vast majority of the mothers in this study were adamant that they would work, even if only part time, once their children started school. Only the older mothers could begin to see that, without training and assistance to break into the jobs market, they were never going to work at anything other than low paid, low skilled service sector jobs:

"We could only do cleaning ... and that don't pay enough, not by the time you pay for baby sitters and that, wouldn't be worth it."

The real training and employment prospects of young single mothers should be studied in detail, and policies developed which will offer suitable training for available job opportunities.

Notes to Part III

1   Finer Committee 1974 *Report of the Committee on One-Parent Families.* Cmnd 5629 HMSO (London)

2   Kempson, E. *et al.* (1994) *Hard times? How poor families make ends meet.* Policy Studies Institute (London)

3   Blake, J. (1994). 'The Impact of CCT on Housing Management', *Roof* May–June